The
Duck
Handbook

Heinz-Sigurd Raethel and Julie R. Mancini

**With full-color photographs
Illustrations by Michele Earle-Bridges**

BARRON'S

Photo Credits

Cover Photos

English language editions © Copyright 2005, 1989 by Barron's Educational Series, Inc.

Original German version entitled *Enten* © Copyright 1988 by Gräfe and Unzer, GmbH, Munich, Germany.

All inquiries should be addressed to:
Barron's Educational Series, Inc.
250 Wireless Boulevard
Hauppauge, New York 11788
www.barronseduc.com

International Standard Book No. 0-7641-3098-6

Library of Congress Catalog Card No. 2005041066

Library of Congress Cataloging-in-Publication Data
Raethel, Heinz-Sigurd.
  [Enten. English]
  The duck handbook / Heinz-Sigurd Raethel and Julie R. Mancini ; illustrations by Michele Earle-Bridges.
    p. cm.
  Rev. ed. of: The new duck handbook. c1989.
  ISBN 0-7641-3098-6
  1. Ducks. I. Mancini, Julie R. (Julie Rach). II. Title.

SF505.R1713 2005
636.5'97—dc22   2005041066

Printed in China
9 8 7 6 5 4 3 2 1

About the Authors

Birds have been an important part of Julie Mancini's life ever since her father built a shelf outside the kitchen window in Culver City, California, on which to feed pigeons. He did this to provide her with mealtime entertainment as a toddler, and she's been hooked on birds ever since. Her mother encouraged her to bird-watch and to appreciate nature, and Julie has seen birds—from chipping sparrows in her backyard to western meadowlarks atop fence posts in Custer State Park in the Dakotas to a bald eagle soaring over Zion National Park in Utah—throughout the western United States.

Julie has been a freelance writer since 1997, with pets as her primary focus. She is the coauthor of Barron's *Guide to Backyard Birds* with her good friend and avian expert, Pamela L. Higdon. Julie and her husband are planning to install a pond on their acreage in central Iowa to attract ducks.

Dr. Heinz-Sigurd Raethel is a retired director of veterinary services and has been a scientific advisor on the board of trustees of the Zoological Garden of Berlin for many years. His major interest has always been ducks, with a special focus on ornamental ducks. He is the author of several books on birds and many publications in scientific journals.

Important Note

This book gives advice on buying, keeping, and breeding ducks. Ducks whose flight is not restricted can wreak havoc in a carefully landscaped pond in a neighbor's garden. Ducks should therefore be rendered flightless (see page 50).

As protection for your own family as well as for others, you should build an adequate fence around your duck pond, especially if there are small children in the household.

For your own peace of mind as well as the safety of your ducks, you should construct a secure outdoor enclosure for them to stay in at night. This enclosure should be fenced with a sturdy fence that is at least 6 feet (1.8 m) high to keep out predators. The bottom of the fence should be reinforced, too, to prevent animals from digging into the enclosure and bothering your birds.

Liability insurance that covers the duck pond is highly recommended.

Any keeper of ducks has to make sure that no water from the pond will drain onto neighboring property, whether above ground or below. It is therefore important to check the drainage pipe regularly and to change the water or empty the pond correctly (see page 52).

Domestic ducks are not allowed on the waters of fish hatcheries and spawning grounds or in nature preserves. Duck keepers who plan to sell duck meat and especially duck eggs should familiarize themselves with pertinent health regulations (see pages 126 and 127).

Any veterinary advice offered in this book is for information only. It is not designed to replace or overrule advice, information, or treatment plans outlined for you by your veterinarian. Your veterinarian is your best duck health resource because he or she knows your birds and their health histories.

Contents

Preface

Ducks are found all over the world and everyone knows what they look like. You may see them on a pond, in a park, on rivers and lakes, or you can go to a zoo to admire the many different beautiful kinds of ducks there are. Duck keepers distinguish between "ornamental" and "utility" or "commercial" ducks. Ornamental ducks are for animal lovers who like having these

Healthy ducks are curious about their surroundings and have bright eyes. Their feathers are well formed, and their feet are smooth and free of calluses.

birds around for their beauty, while utility ducks are kept for the meat, eggs, and down they produce. In this book, the many questions often asked by beginning duck keepers— as well as by those who have had ducks for some time—are answered knowledgeably.

The advice on buying ducks will help you choose the right kind of bird, whether you are interested in breeding, commercial use, or simple enjoyment. Ducks can't do without water, and the chapter Housing and Environment therefore discusses different ways of supplying this basic element, ranging from natural bodies of water to small artificial ponds. Detailed instructions and informative drawings show how to build and equip an artificial duck pond, a duck shelter, and a duck house, as well as an aviary.

Since ducks are omnivorous and far from fussy eaters, picking out a good diet for them from among many possible foods is not difficult. This book also described the different feeding methods appropriate for ornamental ducks, breeding ducks, and market ducks. The chapter Health Care and Diseases describes sicknesses that can occur even among ducks that are fed and cared for properly. The section on breeding ducks includes discussions of the difference between natural and artificial incubation and the hatching and development of ducklings. A special chapter discusses the commercial use of ducks and explains what to do with their meat and eggs.

The chapter on duck behavior describes the rituals of bathing and preening; the molting period, when the ducks are especially vulnerable; the behavior during courtship and between established mates; nest building; and incubation. Accompanying the text are photos that illustrate the "language of ducks." The most popular species of ornamental ducks and the most common utility ducks are introduced in the final chapter. The descriptions of the breeds of utility ducks and species of ornamental ducks include information on origin, appearance, habitat, requirements in captivity, breeding, number of eggs laid, rate of growth, and weight. Many of the ducks described are shown in excellent color photos. A section on showing ducks is also included, as is discussion of some of the problems captive and wild duck populations face in terms of population decline.

Some of you may be wondering why ornamental ducks are classified by species and utility ducks are classified by breeds. Think back to your high school science classes and the lectures on scientific classification that told you that the species was the smallest standard unit of classification. Each ornamental duck belongs to a unique species, while utility ducks are a combination of species that were crossbred for certain traits, such as meat production or egg laying. All utility ducks belong to the same species, *Anas domesticus* (or domestic duck), but they differ in their appearance and characteristics, so they are further classified as breeds of duck, just as all pet dogs belong to the same species, *Canis familiaris* (or domestic dog), but Dachshunds differ from Dalmatians in many ways and are classified as different breeds.

Before we begin, let me take a moment to thank all of those who have contributed to this book, especially Dr. Heinz-Sigurd Raethel, who wrote the first edition of this book, and all of the photographers for supplying their beautiful color photos.

Chapter One
Before You Buy

We don't know how much Walt Disney knew about the nature of real ducks when he created his immortal Donald Duck, along with his entourage of no-less-famous relatives. In any case, this comical bird with its broad bill and even broader behind (the whole tribe is bare-bottomed) has become a symbol of the philistine and the eternal loser without being the least bit unsympathetic.

Ducks have been with us for a long, long time. The word "duck" is derived from the Anglo-Saxon "duce" or "diver," and it dates from the days when the guilt or innocence of suspected witches was tested in a "ducking pond." People were ducking witches before they noticed the ducks bobbing in and out of the water.

Ducks play an important part in our language today. For example, we speak of someone being a sitting duck if he or she is liable to be attacked without warning, or of a politician being a lame duck when he or she is serving out a final term in office. We say that organized people get their ducks in a row in order to get things done, and we say things are just ducky when they are going our way.

Ducks appear in fairy tales only rarely and then as figures of metamorphosis, always in connection, of course, with water. Everyone is familiar with Hans Christian Andersen's story of the "Ugly Duckling" that turns into a beautiful swan. In one of the tales by the Grimm Brothers called "Fundevogel" or "Bird-Foundling," a girl versed in magic transforms her friend into a pond and herself into a duck swimming on the pond. When the evil cook, who sees through the trick, tries to drink the pond dry, the duck grabs her by the head and drags her into the water, where the old witch drowns.

More recently, children around the world have learned important lessons about not trusting strangers after reading Beatrix Potter's *The Tale of Jemima Puddle-Duck*, and they have marveled at the adventures of Mr. and Mrs. Mallard and their offspring Jack, Kack, Lack, Mack, Nack, Ouack, Pack, and

The colorful male mallard.

Quack in Robert McCloskey's classic *Make Way for Ducklings*, which has inspired a statue and an annual parade in Boston's Public Garden. Every May on Mother's Day, children dress up as ducklings and take part in the Duckling Day Parade, following a marching band along the route McCloskey outlined in his book from Beacon Hill to the Public Garden.

People were interested in ducks as early as 2000 B.C., as old pictorial representations show. Ducks were raised and fattened in ancient China, beginning in the Jiangsu Province and moving toward Beijing after it became the country's capital. Ducks were also raised in Egypt and Rome, and Christopher Columbus wrote about flocks of large ducks being kept by natives in the West Indies in the late 1400s.

Ducks have been depicted in the visual arts throughout the ages in various forms: They appear in the spare style of the Egyptians, as an ornamental element in Greek art, as symbols of a feeling for nature in Japanese art, and as striking colorful accents in Dutch genre painting in the 17th century. More recent ducks have been cartoonish and sometimes animated, as in the case of

Walt Disney's Donald and his friends and family, Warner Bros.' Daffy, Hanna-Barbera's Yakky Doodle, and Harvey Comics' Baby Huey.

During World War II, ducks appeared on unit insignia (some of which were drawn by Disney studio animators as part of the war effort) for Allied forces, and military units today still use ducks in their logos. Carved wooden decoys that were originally used in duck hunting have become sought-after collectors' items and are featured in the décor of many homes, even those of non-hunters. Images of ducks have adorned the postage stamps of many countries around the world, catching the eye of bird-watchers as well as stamp collectors. And in the late 1990s, duck keeping became part of pop culture when a family of ducks figured prominently in the first season storyline of the HBO series *The Sopranos*. Mob boss Tony Soprano felt compelled to feed and care for a family of wild ducks that landed in his swimming pool, even as his personal and professional worlds were crumbling around him.

Ornamental or Utility Ducks?

When you decide to keep ducks, you should be clear about what kind of ducks you really want. Duck keepers speak of ornamental and utility or commercial ducks, but what do they mean when they use these terms?

Ornamental ducks, in the language of duck fanciers, means any wild duck species. These ducks are kept as "ornaments" because of their beautiful plumage and their interesting behavior. They are not expected to bring an economic return but are kept strictly for the pleasure of watching them.

Utility or *commercial* ducks are various breeds of domestic ducks. They have been bred by duck fanciers to create birds that are good at laying eggs or producing highly edible meat or useful down feathers. Unlike ornamental duck owners, utility duck owners expect to get an economic return in the form of meat, eggs, and down feathers.

Here are two more specialized terms:
• *Market ducks* are commercial ducks that are being fattened for market.
• *Breeding ducks* are those birds that are kept strictly to produce future generations of ducks.

Ducks for Beginners

As everyone knows, practice makes perfect. The beginning duck keeper should keep this saying in mind as well. Duck enthusiasts should start their new hobby on a modest scale and not take big risks at the beginning. For that reason, this book does not discuss any species or breed that makes difficult demands. There is hardly a more discouraging experience than embarking on a new venture, only to encounter failure. And in the chapter Ornamental Ducks and Utility Ducks (see page 91), you will find which breeds and species are especially

Muscovy ducks are among the quieter duck breeds, which may make them ideal for a suburban setting where their limited noise is less likely to disturb nearby neighbors.

suitable for beginners and what special qualities distinguish them.

Basic Needs

Knowing the basic needs of an animal is a prerequisite for that animal's proper care. Just about everybody knows that ducks are waterfowl and that their essential element is water. Accordingly, all ducks in captivity should have water to swim in to be happy. This is correct in principle. All ornamental and most utility ducks need to be able to swim if they are to survive. But there is no rule without an exception. People have bred some strains, such as the runner, the buff, the Campbell, and the Pekin duck, that can manage without a pond as long as they have opportunities for bathing.

Space Requirements

Ornamental ducks need more space than domestic ducks, so don't make the mistake many beginners make of getting carried away by the beauty of the ducks and buying out of sheer enthusiasm. Always consider first how much space you have available for your future charges. Neither ornamental nor commercial ducks like being crowded together in their runs and shelters with others of their own or related species (see Housing and Environment, page 14). A good rule of thumb is to allow a square yard of interior area for each five ducks to give them adequate room to feel comfortable.

Not all ducks need a pond to swim in, but they all need to be able to bathe as needed.

Duck Care Tips on the Web

Duck keepers with access to the Internet may want to visit these sites for more information on duck care:

- Cornell University's Duck Care Home Page: *www.duckhealth.com*
- Duck Care: *www.newagrarian.com/homestead/ducks/index.html*
- Liveducks.com: *www.liveducks.com*
- The Poultry Site: *www.thepoultrysite.com*
- Quackers Care: *www.poultryconnection.com/quackers/care.html*

To learn more about duck care or to visit sites set up by duck owners and breeders, point your browser toward "pet duck care" or "backyard duck care."

Noise

Noise is one thing a beginning duck fancier hardly ever thinks about ahead of time, and the noise ducks make may well disturb and annoy neighbors. Not many people say, "I like to hear ducks quacking because it reminds me of my childhood in the country." But not all ducks quack constantly and loudly all year-round. Among the ornamental species, only the mallard and the spotbill duck tend to be very noisy; most of the others use their relatively soft voices only during the few weeks of courtship.

Commercial ducks on the whole quack rather loudly. But here, too, there is an exception, the muscovy duck. This utility duck, which was bred from a South American wild species, is almost silent and is guaranteed not to annoy any neighbors.

Time Investment

Looking after ducks does not require a massive time commitment. Chores include daily feeding, clean-

Ducks require about 90 minutes of care a day, including preparing their food, feeding them, and cleaning up after them.

ing the run and, in the winter, the floor of the shelter or house, and changing the water in the swimming basin, which in most cases doesn't have to be done every day. The water has to be changed more frequently only if the basin is very small and the run is crowded. Natural streams and ponds that maintain a biological equilibrium don't require any cleaning at all except for the removal of an occasional dead fish or mouse and other decaying organic matter that may turn up. You should figure on spending an aver-

age of one and a half to two hours a day on your ducks. But keep in mind that this book is intended for amateur and hobby breeders, not for commercial enterprises where birds are kept on a large scale and where, obviously, different rules apply (see Daily Chores, page 51).

Feeding

Neither commercial nor ornamental ducks are difficult to feed. Ducks are omnivores; in fact, they are sometimes referred to as the "pigs of the bird world." If you don't have

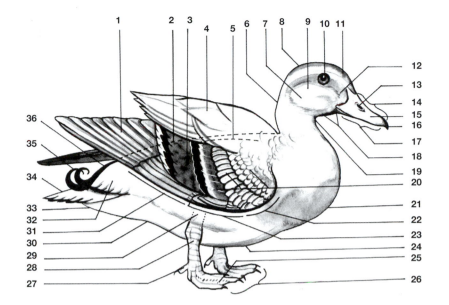

1. primaries
2. back
3. secondaries speculum
4. tertials and scapulars
5. shoulder
6. nape
7. cheek
8. crown
9. ear coverts
10. eye
11. forehead
12. lores
13. nostril

14. culmen or ridge
15. upper mandible
16. nail
17. lower mandible
18. chin
19. throat
20. lesser, median, and
    greater wing coverts
21. breast
22. bend of wing
23. alula
24. abdomen
25. web

26. front toes with claws
27. hind toe
28. tarsus
29. tibiotarsus
30. cloaca
31. primary coverts
32. upper tail coverts
33. under tail coverts
34. tail
35. sex feathers (only in
    drakes)
36. rump

It is important for a duck keeper to know the birds' different body parts.

much time, you can buy commercial rations of various composition for ducklings, breeding ducks, or market ducks and then use them for ornamental as well as utility ducks. If you have more time, you can compose your own duck rations (see Diet, page 29).

Supervision

If for no other reason than self-interest, you will want to keep a watchful eye over your ducks to prevent anything bad from happening to them. This supervision includes making sure that all the birds get their share of food, that the smaller

Mallards are among the ducks that feed on grass and other foodstuffs found in fields and pastures.

and weaker ones are not shoved aside, and that sick birds do not go unnoticed.

Vacation Care

Remember that there may be times when you want to take a vacation away from home. When that happens, you will need to find some kindly person who will take good care of your ducks. But it's not always easy to find such a person, especially at the last minute. So look for a good caretaker for your birds ahead of time, and have him or her do the chores with you for a day or two before you take off for vacation.

Chapter Two

The Basics

The Right Duck for Every Situation

Someone interested in keeping ducks is in the fortunate position of having a great variety to choose from. Whether you are looking for ornamental ducks that will give you esthetic pleasure or whether you are motivated by the more utilitarian desire for meat or eggs, you will almost always find a duck that answers your desires.

For Aesthetic Pleasure

A good way to familiarize yourself with the many different species of ducks and compare them is to visit zoological gardens, which usually have bodies of water populated with many of these waterfowl.

Small species: These, which include the mandarin duck, wood duck, green-winged teal, garganey, Bahama pintail, and Baikal teal, are especially well suited for living in small aviaries and on garden ponds.

Large species: These, which include the pintail, gadwall, falcated teal, red-crested pochard, and the wigeon, should not be crowded together in a small area.

Diving ducks should be avoided unless the body of water you have for them is at least 32 to 40 inches (80 to 100 cm) deep.

For Breeding

If you hope to breed ornamental ducks, don't keep the birds in small, crowded quarters. The fewer pairs that share the limited space of an

A duck preens itself carefully, especially after bathing, to maintain the insulating properties of its plumage. For the feathers to stay water repellent, they have to be arranged properly and oiled frequently with the secretions from the uropygial or oil gland.

A Look at the Law

Before purchasing any ducks for your property, make sure that you can keep them legally. Some cities or developments may have zoning restrictions on certain types of livestock, and it's best to do your research before bringing your first ducks home.

aviary or garden pond, the sooner they are likely to breed (see Keeping Ducks in an Aviary and Keeping Ducks on a Pond, pages 45 and 46).

If you are keeping purebred utility ducks, restrict yourself to one breed per coop or run. It is impossible to obtain purebred offspring if several breeds are kept together. A place to swim is essential for breeding most commercial breeds because they can successfully mate only in the water.

For Commercial Use

Meat is the primary commercial product of ducks, but duck feathers and duck eggs are also useful (see Commercial Uses of Ducks, page 126). Utility ducks are usually exhibited at poultry shows.

How Many Ducks?

Wild or ornamental ducks are monogamous. They are therefore always kept in pairs, although you can house several pairs of the same or related species together.

Domestic or utility ducks have lost their monogamous way of life in the long course of domestication,

and if breeding is the goal, a drake is kept together with several females. Keep no more than five females (called a harem) per drake so that as many of the eggs as possible are fertilized. You should never attempt to house several drakes and their harems together in the same enclosure. The drakes would promptly start fighting over the females, which is bound to have a negative effect on the breeding operation.

Ducklings: The main economic use of ducks is to fatten and sell the ducklings of both sexes. Since these birds are ready for slaughter before they reach sexual maturity, they can all be kept together as long as it is adequate for their numbers. Allow enough room because ducklings that are raised for market grow fast and will soon need quite a bit more space than they did when first hatched or purchased.

Where to Buy Ducks

Feed or farm stores: If you want to purchase ornamental or utility ducks, call feed or farm stores in your area and ask if they sell live birds. The employees can help you select healthy stock and can also recommend proper diets for your birds. You can also order ducklings from virtual farm and feed stores found on the Internet. Have your favorite browser search for "ducklings" or "buy ducks" in order to locate such dealers.

Breeders/hatcheries: In some cases, duck owners are inspired to embark on their hobby after a visit to the duck section of a poultry show. At these exhibitions mostly commercial breeds are shown; ornamental ducks are less often entered. When you see a type of duck you like, you can usually buy some from the breeder who is exhibiting the birds. You can also contact duck hatcheries to purchase ducklings or adult ducks for your home flock.

How to Tell If a Duck Is Healthy

You can assess a duck's state of health by looking for certain signs:

Behavior: A healthy duck looks at the world with bright, lively eyes and tries to get away from people. This is especially true when it has just arrived at its new home.

Plumage: The plumage should be smooth and clean, especially in the vent area. A new duck may be dirty because it soiled itself out of fear during the trip, which should, of course, not be interpreted as a sign of illness.

Feet: The duck's feet should be smooth, and the duck should have no calluses, let alone sores, on the underside of the toes.

State of nutrition: You can judge the state of nutrition by feeling the bird's breast region. The breast muscles should be well developed.

A duck that is sick or improperly nourished has a narrow breastbone that protrudes sharply. However, this test does not work with very young ducklings and recently fledged ducklings because their breast muscles are not yet fully developed at this age, so the breastbone will not be well covered regardless of the state of the bird's nutrition and health.

How to Handle a Duck

Handling a duck takes a little patience and practice, but with gentle repetition, you will become more skilled at handling ducks and your ducks will become easier to handle because they will be accustomed to you picking them up and carrying them.

To pick up a duckling, simply scoop it up in your hand and hold it gently, but firmly, close to your chest. The sound of your heartbeat may help calm the duckling, and having it close to your body will help you control it better if it should become startled and try to fly away.

To pick up an adult duck, approach it from behind and grab it gently so that your hands are over its wings. Holding the bird's wings down will prevent it from flying and will make it easier to handle. Bring the bird toward your body and adjust it so that it fits in the crook of your elbow. Situate your arm so that it supports the duck's body from below because this will help the duck feel more secure while you are holding it. Gently stroke the duck's wings and body with your free hand and talk calmly to it. Let the duck go after a few moments or if it begins to struggle significantly, because you don't want the duck to become overly stressed by the handling. Work with your duck every day to ensure that it remains comfortable with being handled.

The Life Span of Ducks

Ornamental or wild ducks: They can live 12 to 15 years. Most fanciers acquire them as young adult birds when their sex is already obvious from the color of the plumage. But sometimes older ducks that are reliable breeders come up for sale and are worth buying because wild ducks can breed until they are quite old. Still, you should make a practice never to buy any kind of ducks that are more than six years old.

Long-Lived Ducks

Mallards are among the longest-lived ducks in the wild. One bird lived to be 27 years old, and others have lived into their early 20s. The age is determined by bands on the birds' legs that indicate when and where they were banded.

Domestic or commercial ducks are always slaughtered before they reach their potential maximum age.

Generally, commercial ducks are purchased by producers as day-old chicks. If you plan to breed ducks, it is best to buy the birds in the late summer or in the fall because they are strongest then and usually cheapest, too. They should not be more than two years old.

When it comes to the age of fully grown ducks, all you have to go on is the seller's word because you cannot check an adult duck's age. It is always best to deal with reputable breeders.

Transporting Ducks

In most of North America, ducks can be purchased at feed or farm stores. This means that most duck owners will likely bring their stock home from the store in a cardboard box or travel carrier, depending on the number and size of the ducks purchased at any one particular visit to the feed store.

Private breeders are another source for live ducks. In some cases, these breeding facilities may be local, and in others, they may be located in another state or province, which means the ducks may be purchased through an Internet or mail order. In these cases, the live ducks will be shipped via air freight or through the post office in crates or cardboard boxes.

Shipping Containers

When ducks are shipped air freight or by mail, they arrive in crates or cardboard boxes. Because the birds eliminate out of fear during transport, disposable boxes of heavy cardboard are used for short trips. Duck chicks are usually shipped in similar cardboard boxes. If the trip lasts for more than a day, ducks will be shipped in a pet travel carrier so that the birds will not be injured during transport. The crates should not be too roomy, so that if the birds panic and start dashing around frantically, they cannot injure themselves or trample each other to death. If several birds are to be shipped together, it may be safer to subdivide a large crate so that each duck has its own compartment. Ducklings are usually shipped in compartmentalized cardboard boxes that hold five chicks apiece.

The Shipping Container

If your duck arrives by air freight or by mail, you will notice a few things about the shipping container. A shipping container for live animals must have enough large round air holes to keep the animals inside from suffocating. The bottom should consist of an absorbent material, such as several thicknesses of filter paper with a layer of straw on top. A large label with the words "Caution! Live poultry!" in easily legible lettering should be securely affixed to the outside of the container to alert shipping personnel to the contents.

Method of Shipping

For short distances, the birds should be shipped at night if at all possible. If your ducks will arrive through the mail, arrange to have them shipped overnight in order to track the shipment in case it gets misdirected. Have the breeder inform you when the ducks are due to arrive so you will be available to meet the mailman and receive your shipment promptly.

Arrival at the Destination

Before you accept a shipment, check that the animals are alive and well and that they are the species or breed you ordered. If your birds arrive in poor health or dead, inform the breeder immediately so steps can be taken to rectify the situation.

Unpacking

After you unpack the ducks, clean off the soiled and sticky parts of the plumage with a soft sponge and lukewarm water. The ducks themselves will later do a thorough cleaning of their plumage. If the new arrivals are the sole occupants of the shelter and run, and if the weather is clement, you can release the ducks immediately into their new home, assuming that they look healthy. Watch them swim for a while to make sure that their plumage is properly water repellent so that they won't drown (see Dry Plumage, page 57).

Chapter Three

Housing and Environment

An Artificial Duck Pond

It makes sense to build your duck pond somewhere where you can conveniently watch your ducks. This is usually near a terrace or a window. Although it might seem kinder for the ducks, a spot underneath trees is not recommended. First of all, removing dead leaves in the fall is a major chore; a more serious consideration is that the pressure of tree roots (especially of fast-growing species) may cause leaks in the pond walls. I would therefore urge you to pick a sunny but protected location.

You can choose to build your pond with either concrete or heavy plastic walls. The following sections give you some general advice on constructing ponds, and you can find more detailed instructions in some of the books listed in For Further Reading, on page 132.

Ponds Made of Concrete

Preparation: Mark the outlines of the pond with wooden stakes in the exact spot where you plan to locate the pond. Two pairs of ornamental ducks should have a pond measuring about 30 to 40 square feet (3 to 4 sq m). When establishing the depth of the pond, remember to consider the water depth needed by the ducks plus the thickness of the concrete bottom. You will have to dig down
- at least 24 inches plus 14 inches (60 cm plus 35 cm) for dabbling ducks, and
- 40 plus 14 inches (1 m plus 35 cm) for diving ducks.

Gently slope one side of the pond so the ducks can climb in and out of the water easily. Pound the bottom of the hole for the pond smooth and hard all over. Remove large rocks and thick roots because they might later cause cracks in the concrete. If the soil is too loose, cover it with gravel or broken bricks, then stamp them into the ground.

Pouring the concrete: You make concrete by mixing 1 part dry Portland cement with 5 parts sand, then add enough water mixed with a sealer to get the consistency of stiff dough. The usual proportion of sealer to water is 1 to 30. Build the

Duck ponds can be either natural or man-made. Take advantage of naturally occurring water on your property to attract ducks, or create a pond on your property to provide a place for ducks to rest, eat, and preen.

layers of concrete up to 6 inches (15 cm), working in strips or "forms" rather than covering the entire area all at once. Smooth the surface with a board. Since wet concrete tends not to keep its shape on sloping walls, place a layer of wire mesh over it to give it a solid "corset." In some places, strips of wire mesh will overlap, so weigh these seams down with bricks. Then add a second 6-inch (15-cm) layer of the cement; smooth it and remove the bricks on the seams as you go along. To prevent the concrete from drying too quickly, cover each form immediately with damp sand, and spread damp cloths over the edges of the pond. Keep both the sand and the cloths damp, and don't remove them until the concrete has set. Finally, fill in the pores of the rough concrete walls with mortar (1 part cement to 3 parts

sand with enough water to make a spreadable mixture), and smooth the surface with a board.

The drain: Ducks dirty the water, and you must replenish it continually. Therefore, a good drain is essential. When you pour the concrete walls of the pond, set a 3-inch (7.6-cm) drainpipe with a brass-screw fitting in the deepest spot. Lay the drainpipe at a downward angle and connect it to the sewage system. (Seek the advice of a plumber for this job.) When you're ready to fill the pond, screw an overflow pipe into the fitting at the bottom. This overflow pipe has a perforated cap or is covered with screening, and it helps avoid flooding when the water surface rises (such as after a heavy rain), and the drain stays clear of feathers, leaves, or larger particles of dirt. If you live in an area where frost

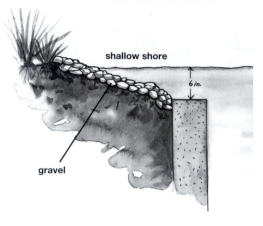

shallow shore

6 in.

gravel

When building a duck pond, the edge of the pond should be made very shallow on one side and covered with gravel.

is a problem, drain the pond for the winter to prevent frost damage.

Ponds Made of Plastic

The great advantage of plastic over concrete is that it can expand and will consequently not suffer frost damage. Also, you do not need to drain a plastic pond during the winter.

Preparation: Excavate the site of the pond just as you would for a concrete pond. Clean the surface carefully and smooth it because pointed objects can damage the plastic. Make sure the place where the ducks get in and out has a very slight slope because the plastic can become extremely slippery when algae develop on it. Use plastic designed exclusively for building ponds. (This kind of liner—usually made of butyl plastic or PVC—is available at pond specialty stores, at garden centers, and at some pet-supply stores.) The plastic comes in

rolls of different widths and should be at least 0.03 inch (0.75 mm) thick. Calculate ahead of time how much plastic you need and take into account that the plastic has to reach about 1 foot (30 cm) beyond the edges of the pool.

Putting down the plastic: If a single sheet of plastic is not large enough for the entire pond, you will have to glue strips of plastic together with a chemical that welds the edges together. Ask a salesperson where you are buying the plastic for advice.

Spread out the plastic next to the excavation for the pond and carefully pull it over the hole, making sure that the protruding rim is about the same width all around (about 12 inches [30 cm]). Then start running water slowly into the pond. The water will press the plastic tightly into the excavation. Wait two or three days after you've filled the pond before you fix the edges with flat rocks.

Drainpipe: The drainpipe is installed in the same way as it is in a concrete pond, but it has to be carefully welded to the plastic before filling the pond with water.

Shaping the Pond's Edge

To make the pond look more natural in its setting, cover the edges with natural stones, except for the flat sections where the ducks climb in and out. Pieces of slate, limestone flags, or plain, flat rocks work well. Take care to use only smooth stones to avoid injuring your ducks' feet on sharp stones or gravel at the pond's edge. If your pond has concrete walls, you can set the rocks into the top of the walls. With plastic ponds, lay them on the protruding rim of plastic.

Planting the Pond and Its Surroundings

A new keeper of ornamental ducks often wants to recreate a natural habitat by planting marsh and water plants in and around the duck pond. But if you think you can transform your pond into a natural-looking landscape complete with water lilies, reeds, rushes, frogs, fish, and turtles, you are in for an unpleasant surprise. A duck has only one thing on its mind, and that is to search for food as assiduously as possible. A charmingly planted pond with just one pair of ducks on it will soon lose its aesthetic appeal. Torn-off leaves and water lily blossoms will soon be floating on the water's surface, the frogs will disappear, the fish will retreat to hidden corners, and the water turtles' quiet way of life will be disrupted.

Still, it is possible to have a decorative green plant cover on the pond by planting duckweed. This plant will thrive, though you may have to add a few bucketfuls from time to time. And you can also incorporate some shrubbery and green grass into the surrounding landscape. But protect your flowering perennials and flower beds from the voracious appetite of the ducks with a low chicken-wire fence.

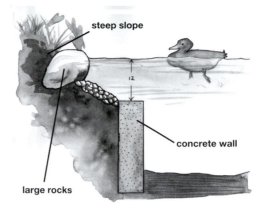

Building a steep shore of large rocks will secure you against mudslides. Set the rocks into the ground at a slightly upward angle.

Plants for the duck run: Some reasonably indestructible plants that can be planted to provide greenery in place of a lawn are ground ivy (*Glechomá hederacea*), silverweed (*Potentilla anserina*), various chamomile species (*Matricaria*), and for a larger plant, the large-leafed butterbur (*Petasites*).

Plants for the edge of the pond: Some taller flowering plants and decorative grasses that ducks don't eat are day lilies (*Hemerocallis*), yellow iris (*Iris pseudacorus*), *Arundinaria* bamboo plants, the tall perennial grass eulalia (*Miscanthus*), and in milder climates, the magnificent pampas grass (*Cotaderia*).

Protection for nests: Ornamental ducks like to build their nests in the dense foliage of stinging nettle (*Urtica dioica*), butterbur (*Petasites*), and smartweed (*Polygonum hydropiper*).

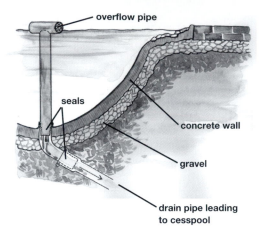

overflow pipe

seals

concrete wall

gravel

drain pipe leading
to cesspool

*Building a drainage pipe with an overflow
pipe attached is strongly recommended
if you're building your own duck pond.
The drainage pipe should in turn be
attached to the sewage system on your
property. Be sure to consult an expert
before tapping into the sewage system.*

A Natural Duck Pond

Natural ponds are excellent for ornamental as well as for commercial ducks if they are not polluted by household sewage or industrial effluents. Check the water quality carefully before releasing ducks into the pond because polluted water can poison them. If you find fish swimming around actively, this is a good indication that the water is suitable for ducks as well. To keep the ducks from escaping, enclose the pond and the area around it with a wire-mesh fence.

Carp ponds are also ideal for keeping utility ducks. The fast-growing and productive Pekin ducks can be kept this way. One side benefit is that duck dung fertilizes the pond organically, which leads to rapid plankton growth. The plankton means that the carp have more food and therefore grow faster. The maximum number of ducks that should be kept on a 1-acre area of water is about 100.

Keeping ornamental ducks on larger ponds with natural vegetation is ideal in theory, but you have to be braced for losses caused by martens, dogs, and cats because ornamental ducks, to keep them from flying away, have to have their wings clipped (see Rendering Ducks Flightless, page 50). Small species, such as the green-winged teal, garganey, and Baikal teal, cannot be kept on such waters if you cannot keep an eye on them, because they would

Protection from wind and sun: Low-growing conifers, such as Chinese juniper (*Juniperus chinensis pfitzeriana*) and dwarf pine (*Pinus mugo pumilio*), serve this function well. Ducks don't nibble on them but use their shade to rest in and find hidden places among them for building their nests.

When you visit duck breeders and zoological gardens, examine their duck areas and take a close look at the shrubs and bushes growing near the duck ponds. Any plants that thrive there are likely to do well in or around your pond. Also ask for recommendations at the pond specialty store where you bought your building supplies, because the staff there is likely to know which plants will grow well in your area.

soon wander off, never to be seen again.

Problems also occur when the water begins to freeze. That is why at some point in the fall you should begin feeding your ornamental ducks in a wire cage with a door that can be raised and lowered. They get used to it quite quickly. Then, when the water first begins to ice over, you close the door while the ducks are eating and move them to a barn with an attached aviary, where they spend the winter. Many parks use this method to winter over their swans.

If you live near a fish hatchery or protected wildlife area, duck keeping may not be permitted, since ducks like to eat fish eggs and fry. In protected wildlife areas they also threaten tadpoles, rare aquatic plants, and the eggs of amphibians.

Other unsuitable duck homes are standing bodies of water without inlets or outlets and small, dirty puddles. In such waters, lack of oxygen often leads to decomposition processes during hot, dry summers, and ducks may die of botulism poisoning (see Botulism, page 58).

Wild Ducks

Duck ponds and duck yards can be virtual magnets for wild ducks, which offer duck keepers the opportunity to observe wild ducks and compare and contrast their behavior with the ducks they keep.

Following are a list of wild duck species seen in North America and a list of the regions and/or provinces where they may be seen.

The United States is divided into the following regions:

Pacific (Alaska, Washington, Oregon, California, Nevada, and Hawaii)

Mountain (Idaho, Montana, Wyoming, Colorado, Utah, Arizona, and New Mexico)

West North Central (North Dakota, South Dakota, Minnesota, Iowa, Missouri, Nebraska, and Kansas)

West South Central (Oklahoma, Texas, Arkansas, and Louisiana)

East South Central (Mississippi, Alabama, Tennessee, and Kentucky)

East North Central (Wisconsin, Illinois, Indiana, Ohio, and Michigan)

Middle Atlantic (New York, New Jersey, and Pennsylvania)

South Atlantic (Delaware, District of Columbia, Maryland, Virginia, West Virginia, North Carolina, South Carolina, Georgia, and Florida)

New England (Maine, New Hampshire, Vermont, Massachusetts, Rhode Island, and Connecticut)

The provinces of Canada are as follows: Alberta, British Columbia, Manitoba, New Brunswick, Newfoundland and Labrador, Northwest Territories, Nova Scotia, Nunavut, Ontario, Prince Edward Island, Quebec, Saskatchewan, and Yukon.

American black duck: West South Central, East South Central, East North Central, Middle Atlantic, South Atlantic, New England; Saskatchewan, Manitoba, Ontario, Quebec, Newfoundland, New Brunswick, Prince Edward Island, Nova Scotia.

Canvasback ducks are commonly seen on ponds and lakes throughout the United States and Canada.

American wigeon: Pacific, Mountain, West North Central, West South Central, East South Central, Middle Atlantic, South Atlantic, New England; Yukon, Northwest Territories, British Columbia, Alberta, Saskatchewan, Manitoba, Ontario, Quebec, Newfoundland, New Brunswick, Prince Edward Island, Nova Scotia.

Barrow's goldeneye: Pacific, Mountain, New England; Yukon, Northwest Territories, British Columbia, Quebec, Newfoundland, New Brunswick, Prince Edward Island, Nova Scotia.

Black scoter: Pacific, West South Central, Middle Atlantic, South Atlantic, New England; Yukon, Northwest Territories, British Columbia, Alberta, Saskatchewan, Manitoba, Ontario, Quebec, Newfoundland, New Brunswick, Prince Edward Island, Nova Scotia.

Blue-winged teal: Pacific, West South Central, East South Central, South Atlantic; Yukon, Northwest Territories, British Columbia, Alberta,

Saskatchewan, Manitoba, Ontario, Quebec, Newfoundland, New Brunswick, Prince Edward Island, Nova Scotia.

Bufflehead: Pacific, Mountain, West South Central, East South Central, East North Central, Middle Atlantic, South Atlantic, New England; Yukon, Northwest Territories, British Columbia, Alberta, Saskatchewan, Manitoba, Ontario, Quebec, Newfoundland, New Brunswick, Prince Edward Island, Nova Scotia.

Canvasback: Pacific, West South Central, East South Central, East North Central, Middle Atlantic, South Atlantic; Yukon, Northwest Territories, British Columbia, Alberta, Saskatchewan, Manitoba, Ontario, Quebec, Newfoundland, New Brunswick, Prince Edward Island, Nova Scotia.

Cinnamon teal: Pacific, Mountain; Yukon, Northwest Territories, British Columbia, Alberta, Saskatchewan, Manitoba, Ontario, Quebec, New Brunswick, Nova Scotia.

Common eider: Alaska, New England; Yukon, Northwest Territories, British Columbia, Alberta, Saskatchewan, Manitoba, Ontario, Quebec, Newfoundland, New Brunswick, Prince Edward Island, Nova Scotia.

Common goldeneye: Pacific, Mountain, West North Central, West South Central, East South Central, East North Central, Middle Atlantic, South Atlantic, New England; Yukon, Northwest Territories, British Columbia, Alberta, Saskatchewan, Manitoba, Ontario, Quebec, Newfoundland,

New Brunswick, Prince Edward Island, Nova Scotia.

Common merganser: Pacific, Mountain, West North Central, East North Central, Middle Atlantic, South Atlantic, New England; Yukon, Northwest Territories, British Columbia, Alberta, Saskatchewan, Manitoba, Ontario, Quebec, Newfoundland, New Brunswick, Prince Edward Island, Nova Scotia.

Eurasian teal: Quebec.

Eurasian wigeon: Yukon, Northwest Territories, British Columbia, Alberta, Saskatchewan, Manitoba, Ontario, Quebec, Newfoundland, New Brunswick, Prince Edward Island, Nova Scotia.

Fulvous whistling-duck: West South Central, South Atlantic; British Columbia, Alberta, Ontario, Quebec, New Brunswick, Prince Edward Island, Nova Scotia.

Gadwall: Pacific, Mountain, West North Central, West South Central, East South Central, South Atlantic; Yukon, Northwest Territories, British Columbia, Alberta, Saskatchewan, Manitoba, Ontario, Quebec, Newfoundland, New Brunswick, Prince Edward Island, Nova Scotia.

Greater scaup: Pacific, West South Central, East North Central, Middle Atlantic, South Atlantic, New England; Yukon, Northwest Territories, British Columbia, Alberta, Saskatchewan, Manitoba, Ontario, Quebec, Newfoundland, New Brunswick, Prince Edward Island, Nova Scotia.

Green-winged teal: Pacific, Mountain, West North Central, West

The European or Eurasian wigeon can be found throughout Canada.

South Central, East South Central, South Atlantic; Yukon, Northwest Territories, British Columbia, Alberta, Saskatchewan, Manitoba, Ontario, Quebec, Newfoundland, New Brunswick, Prince Edward Island, Nova Scotia.

Harlequin duck: Pacific, New England; Yukon, Northwest Territories, British Columbia, Alberta, Saskatchewan, Manitoba, Ontario, Quebec, Newfoundland, New Brunswick, Prince Edward Island, Nova Scotia.

Hooded merganser: Pacific, West South Central, East South Central, East North Central, South Atlantic, New England; Yukon, Northwest Territories, British Columbia, Alberta, Saskatchewan, Manitoba, Ontario, Quebec, Newfoundland,

New Brunswick, Prince Edward Island, Nova Scotia.

King eider: Alaska, Middle Atlantic, New England; Yukon, Northwest Territories, British Columbia, Alberta, Saskatchewan, Ontario, Quebec, Newfoundland, New Brunswick, Prince Edward Island, Nova Scotia.

Lesser scaup: Pacific, Mountain, West South Central, East South Central, South Atlantic; Yukon, Northwest Territories, British Columbia, Alberta, Saskatchewan, Manitoba, Ontario, Quebec, Newfoundland, New Brunswick, Prince Edward Island, Nova Scotia.

Mallard: Pacific, Mountain, West North Central, West South Central, East South Central, East North Central, Middle Atlantic, South Atlantic, New England; Yukon, Northwest Territories, British Columbia, Alberta, Saskatchewan, Manitoba, Ontario, Quebec, Newfoundland, New Brunswick, Prince Edward Island, Nova Scotia.

The lesser scaup is one of the most commonly seen ducks on lakes and bays across Canada and the United States.

Masked duck: West South Central.

Muscovy duck: West South Central.

Northern pintail: Yukon, Northwest Territories, British Columbia, Alberta, Saskatchewan, Manitoba, Ontario, Quebec, Newfoundland, New Brunswick, Prince Edward Island, Nova Scotia.

Northern shoveler: Pacific, Mountain, West North Central, West South Central, East North Central, South Atlantic; Yukon, Northwest Territories, British Columbia, Alberta, Saskatchewan, Manitoba, Ontario, Quebec, Newfoundland, New Brunswick, Prince Edward Island, Nova Scotia.

Oldsquaw or Long-tailed duck: Pacific, West South Central, East South Central, East North Central, Middle Atlantic, South Atlantic, New England; Yukon, Northwest Territories, British Columbia, Alberta, Saskatchewan, Manitoba, Ontario, Quebec, Newfoundland, New Brunswick, Prince Edward Island, Nova Scotia.

Red-breasted merganser: Pacific, West South Central, East South Central, East North Central, Middle Atlantic, South Atlantic, New England; Yukon, Northwest Territories, British Columbia, Alberta, Saskatchewan, Manitoba, Ontario, Quebec, Newfoundland, New Brunswick, Prince Edward Island, Nova Scotia.

Redhead: Pacific, Mountain, West North Central, East North Central; Yukon, Northwest Territories, British

The northern shoveler uses its bill to filter foods from the water. Its range includes much of Canada and the western United States.

Columbia, Alberta, Saskatchewan, Manitoba, Ontario, Quebec, Newfoundland, New Brunswick, Prince Edward Island, Nova Scotia.

Ring-necked duck: Pacific, Mountain, West South Central, East South Central, Middle Atlantic, South Atlantic, New England; Yukon, Northwest Territories, British Columbia, Alberta, Saskatchewan, Manitoba, Ontario, Quebec, Newfoundland, New Brunswick, Prince Edward Island, Nova Scotia.

Ruddy duck: Pacific, Mountain, West North Central, West South Central, East South Central, East North Central, Middle Atlantic, South Atlantic; Yukon, Northwest Territories, British Columbia, Alberta, Saskatchewan, Manitoba, Ontario, Quebec, Newfoundland, New Brunswick, Prince Edward Island, Nova Scotia.

Ruddy shelduck: Nova Scotia.

Smew: Alaska, British Columbia, Ontario, Quebec.

Spectacled eider: Alaska, Northwest Territories, British Columbia.

Spot-billed duck: Alaska.

Steller's eider: Alaska, Northwest Territories, British Columbia, Quebec.

Surf scoter: Pacific, West South Central, Middle Atlantic, South Atlantic, New England; Yukon, Northwest Territories, British Columbia, Alberta, Saskatchewan, Manitoba,

The surf scoter is a common sight along the east and west coasts of the United States.

During cold weather, bring ducks into a sheltered area to protect them from extreme temperatures. You can create a duck shelter in the corner of a barn for such occasions.

Ontario, Quebec, Newfoundland, New Brunswick, Prince Edward Island, Nova Scotia.

Tufted duck: Pacific, New England; Yukon, British Columbia, Alberta, Saskatchewan, Ontario, Quebec, Newfoundland, New Brunswick, Prince Edward Island, Nova Scotia.

White-winged scoter: Pacific, West South Central, Middle Atlantic, South Atlantic, New England; Yukon, Northwest Territories, British Columbia, Alberta, Saskatchewan, Manitoba, Ontario, Quebec, Newfoundland, New Brunswick, Prince Edward Island, Nova Scotia.

Wood duck: Pacific, West North Central, West South Central, East South Central, East North Central, Middle Atlantic, South Atlantic, New England; Yukon, British Columbia, Alberta, Saskatchewan, Manitoba, Ontario, Quebec, Newfoundland, New Brunswick, Prince Edward Island, Nova Scotia.

The Duck Shelter

Both ornamental and commercial ducks require shelter from the cold of winter. On sunny winter days, let the ducks outside. Since they are fed inside the shelter, they will return there in the evening of their own accord. On farms, utility ducks frequently spend the winter in empty chicken coops or pigpens.

Requirements for Housing

Method of Construction and Size

A shelter for ornamental and/or commercial ducks is usually built of wood and is supported by a foundation of cinderblocks or concrete. This is the only way to protect the wood from the moisture in the ground and thus to keep it from rotting. A foundation also makes it harder for rats and predators, such as fox and marten, to get into the shelter. Site the shelter so that the inside gets as much light as possible, which means that the front should face south or southeast.

The size of the shelter depends primarily on your desires and constraints. A space 6 feet wide, 4 feet deep, and 5 feet, 8 inches high (2 × 1.2 × 1.7 m) is sufficient to accommodate one or two pairs of ducks. The foundation should extend 20 inches (50 cm) down into the ground and rise 4 inches (10 cm) above it. Build the walls with boards on both sides of the studs and insulate them with foam. The structure is usually covered with a shed roof that slopes down toward the back. It should extend somewhat more over the front of the building than over the sides to keep the rain out.

Floor and Bedding

The floor of the shelter should consist of a 5- to 6-inch (12- to 15-cm) layer of broken brick or gravel, onto which 2½ to 3 inches (6 to 8 cm) of concrete is poured and smoothed; such a concrete floor is easy to clean and disinfect. Then put down a thick layer of sand, peat moss, or sawdust for bedding. When the bedding gets dirty, it is easy to clean out. If it is very cold, put a layer of straw on top.

Temperature

Most ornamental and all commercial ducks are quite hardy and are not bothered if the temperature drops a few degrees below freezing—after all, they are equipped with a warm, thick down coat. Tropical ducks sometimes freeze their toes and webs when it gets very cold. To keep the shelter warm enough, install a heat lamp on the ceiling.

Windows and Doors

To let in as much light as possible, the shelter should have a large window with the kind of glass used

Building Ordinances

Before you start building your duck shelter, check to be sure that your plans conform to any local building ordinances that may be in effect. Generally, all permanent structures, regardless of size, have to be approved. It is therefore a good idea to notify local authorities, such as the official in charge of issuing building permits in your city or town, of your plans. If you want to build on leased land, you will first have to ask the landowner's permission.

in gardening for cold frames. White-wash the inside walls every year. A door next to the window connects the shelter to the run and pond or to the aviary. A second door is useful so that you don't have to walk through the outdoor run or aviary every time the ducks need to be fed or their house cleaned.

Food and Water Dishes, Swimming Basin

Ducks have a habit of softening the food they are about to eat by dip-ping their full bills into their drinking water. This means that the floor soon gets very messy. To minimize the mess, set food and water dishes on a rack mounted on a low platform.

It is important, especially for diving ducks, that they have a place to swim even inside the shelter. A galvanized tub can be used for this purpose. It can be sunk into the floor or made accessible for the ducks by means of a small ladder. Drain the dirty water to the outside, where the ground can absorb it. It is often necessary to change the water every day.

A Large Duck House

If you plan to breed or raise ducks for the market, you will need a larger setup. The duck house described here is adequate for a maximum of 40 breeding ducks or 80 ducklings to be raised for market.

Construction Plan

The structure described here is 13 feet, 1 inch (4 m) wide, and 16 feet, 5 inches (5 m) long and rests on a cinderblock or concrete founda-tion. Prepare the floor the same way as for a small shelter (see page 25). The wooden walls are 40 inches (1 m) high, and the ridge of the gable roof is 75 inches (1.9 m) off the floor. There are two windows, 40 inches (1 m) wide and 20 inches (.5 m) high, in each side wall and four small doors just above ground level with open-ings 10 × 10 inches (25 × 25 cm) leading into the outdoor runs.

On the gable end facing away from the prevailing wind, there is a 70- × 35-inch (180- × 90-cm) door, and a walkway 35 inches (90 cm) wide leading down the middle of the building. You can feed and water the birds, as well as clean the four com-partments on each side easily from this center walkway. Each compart-ment is 6 feet, 5 inches (2 m) long and 3 feet, 2½ inches (1 m) wide and can accommodate one breeding unit of commercial ducks consisting of one drake and four hens.

Fattening ducks: If you want to raise ducks for market, take down the low (24 inches or 60 cm) wooden walls that separate the compart-ments. Now you have an area of 172 square feet (16 sq m) for your ducks. The standard space requirement for 20 newly hatched ducklings is about 11 square feet (1 sq m) during the first two weeks. During the third to fifth week, the same space will be adequate for only 8 to 10 ducklings, and from the sixth to the eighth week, only 4 to 5 birds can be con-tained in that space.

Dabbling ducks such as mallards brood their ducklings for three or four weeks. The ducklings make their first attempts at flying when they are between seven and eight weeks of age.

Food and Water

Feeders and waterers are located on the wall bordering the walkway and should be placed on a wire-covered platform. This is to reduce soaking of the bedding as much as possible. Ducks like to spill water. A drainage channel that runs through all the compartments along the walkway is a useful feature. Small gates in the wall along the walkway provide access to the compartments for cleaning.

Temperature

The temperature in the duck quarters should not rise above 77°F (25°C) in the summer, and it should not drop below freezing in the winter. Air humidity should not be too high because high humidity slows down egg laying. That is why there should be air vents at the ridge of the roof to ensure adequate ventilation.

Outdoor Runs

Ducks should stay indoors only at night and when the weather is very cold; the rest of the time they should be out. Each compartment is therefore connected to a run the birds can get to through a small door. The runs should be separated from each other by a 16-inch (40-cm) chicken-wire fence. There should be a water channel, made of concrete, 32 inches wide by 16 inches deep (80 cm wide × 40 cm deep) running through all the runs at the far end from the duck house to give the ducks a chance to swim.

An Aviary for Ducks

An aviary is a space for birds that is enclosed on all sides, including the top, with grating or wire mesh, and that is large enough for the occupants to use their wings for flying. Usually only ornamental ducks are kept in aviaries. For small species, the aviary provides safety from predators, and many ornamental ducks can be pure-bred only in aviaries because they are likely to hybridize otherwise.

Construction

Situate the aviary so that it gets sunshine at least part of the day, and construct it so that it keeps predators out. Digging the wire mesh into the ground a couple of inches is not enough to keep out foxes and martens, which can dig under the wire. An aviary, just like a duck shelter (see page 25), should have a foundation made of cinderblocks or concrete. It should be 16 inches (40 cm) thick, be dug 20 inches (50 cm) into the ground, and rise 12 inches (30 cm) above the ground.

Wire mesh: The wire mesh is held up by metal posts that are set into the concrete. Instead of posts, use metal brackets with U-shaped clamps into which wooden posts can be fitted and fastened with screws.

Use a fine wire mesh intended for use with chicks. The gaps in the weave should be ½ inch (1.25 cm) or no more than ¾ inch (2 cm)—small enough to keep even sparrows out. Hardware cloth, which is made of wire welded into squares, looks very attractive. Don't stretch the wire mesh ceiling too tightly—it should sag slightly so that it will give a little

if your ducks fly and bump into it in their steep take-off pattern.

Floor: Include a swimming basin on the aviary floor. Because ducks carry quite a bit of water with them when they leave the swimming basin, the surrounding floor has to have good drainage; otherwise, the bottom of the aviary will soon turn into a bog of wet mud. When you build the aviary, dig down 20 inches (50 cm) and fill the excavation with a layer of coarse gravel, one of fine gravel, and a top layer of sand.

Decorating

Any aviary looks more attractive if it is landscaped. A log placed horizontally behind the swimming basin and a few erratic boulders of various sizes arranged in a natural pattern enhance the looks of an aviary. Trying to incorporate greenery into an aviary inhabited by ducks is often a vain enterprise. Ornamental ducks confined to a small area tend to ravage plants—but don't give up too quickly. Try a few different kinds of plants (see Planting the Pond and Its Surroundings, page 17). Nest sites are set up in the back of the aviary. For ducks like the wood duck and the mandarin duck, which like to nest in tree holes, these sites should be located at least 20 inches (50 cm) above the ground and made accessible for the birds by way of a slanted log or small ladder.

Chapter Four

Diet

Like chickens, ducks are omnivorous. But because their senses of taste and smell are more discriminating, they are more particular than chickens about what they eat. Their nutritional requirements also vary depending on their stage of development and on the changing seasons of the year. An organism that is still growing needs different food from one that has reached sexual maturity and may be producing eggs. All this has to be taken into account if ducks are to be fed properly.

Digestion

To get a better idea of what ducks should eat, first familiarize yourself with a duck's alimentary canal and how it functions.

Food intake: The bill and tongue serve to pick up food, which is lubricated by secretions from the salivary glands on the inside of the bill and on the tongue so that it can slide down the gullet or esophagus. A widening in the esophagus at the lower end has a function similar to that of a chicken's crop, namely to regulate how much food enters the stomach at any one time. The food that is swallowed collects at the bottom of the gullet and is then passed on in small portions to the proventriculus, the glandular or true stomach of a bird. The lining of the proventriculus is covered with glands that produce thick mucus and gastric juices containing hydrochloric acid and pepsin, substances that break down protein. Beneath the lining there is a thick layer of muscles that propel the food to the gizzard by means of rhythmic contractions.

Grinding the food down: The walls of the gizzard, too, are made up of a thick layer of muscle and a lining containing glands. The secretion of these glands hardens on the inner surface of the gizzard, forming two plates that rub against each other. Every 20 seconds, the walls of the gizzard contract, pressing the two plates together. Since ducks also swallow grains of quartz sand, or grit (see page 36), all the hard components of the food are crushed. This mechanical rubbing action is a kind of substitute for teeth.

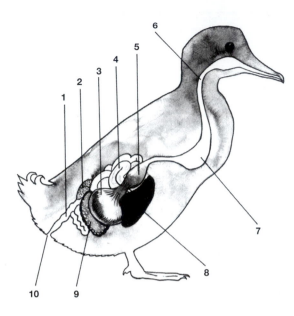

1. large intestine
2. caeca
3. gizzard
4. small intestine
5. proventriculus
6. gullet or esophagus
7. croplike widening of the gullet
8. liver
9. pancreas
10. cloaca

This drawing shows the internal organs of a duck. Ducks are omnivorous and have digestive organs that grind up even very hard foods.

Absorbing nutrients: The food that has thus been "masticated" then goes through a passage from the gizzard into the duodenum. The pancreas and the bile ducts open into the small intestine, contributing secretions that continue the digestive process of the food pulp. Nutrients that are broken down into chemical elements that can be assimilated by the organism are then absorbed through the intestinal lining and enter the bloodstream. A similar process goes on in the large intestine. The caeca, two long, blind tubes similar to our appendix, branch off from the large intestine. Their main function is to produce bacteria that break down cellulose, thus releasing its food value in a form usable by the organism.

The large intestine widens toward the posterior end and forms a roundish chamber, the cloaca. As in all other birds, the alimentary canal as well as the urinary and reproductive canals empty into the cloaca.

Complete Rations and Feeds

Most duck keepers will feed their birds a pelleted or complete diet. These diets, which are available in many feed stores, are scientifically composed feed mixtures that contain all the essential nutrients, including vitamins and trace elements. These rations are sold in the form of meals and pellets. Using them not only simplifies keeping ducks for the beginner but also helps prevent major feeding mistakes.

Pelleted feeds are made of meal mixed with sticky substances such as molasses or cod-liver oil and subjected to high pressure to make them cohere in pellet form. These nutritionally complete pelleted feeds are used almost exclusively in large operations because this feeding method is very simple and therefore economical.

Grains such as barley and rye, which are very healthy but are not eaten enthusiastically by ducks because of their hardness and pointed shape, are readily consumed in pellet form. When you buy pelleted feed, check the size of the pellets: Young ducklings should get smaller pellets, older ducks, larger ones. Pelleted diets present two drawbacks to duck keepers: They may be more expensive than other forms of feed, and if the birds live under crowded conditions (as when raised for market), pelleted feeds may aggravate the tendency of ducks to feather eating.

Commercial feed mixes for poultry generally come in the form of mixed grains, feeds for rearing chicks and for layers, as well as in the form of nutritionally complete rations, either as pellets or as loose meals.

Note: If you feed a commercial mix, try to buy one that's made specifically for ducks or waterfowl. Commercial mixes for chickens or other poultry sometimes contain medications that can be harmful to ducks. If you can't find waterfowl food, purchase nonmedicated chicken pellets or mash for your ducks.

Creating Your Own Duck Diet

If you choose to create your own duck diet, the overview of the digestive system presented earlier in this chapter should help you decide on the makeup of your ducks' diet. Keep in mind that ducks eat foods from two sources: vegetable and animal.

Foods from Vegetable Sources

The various cereal grains are one of the most important food items for commercial as well as ornamental ducks. The food value of grain consists of carbohydrates and proteins in the endosperm (the part of the kernel that is used to make white flour) and fats in the germ. All these nutrients are easily digestible and are present in varying amounts in all grains.

Ducks eat grain in the following order of preference: corn, wheat, barley, oats, and rye. To make sure that the birds don't pick out one kind and leave the rest, be sure to mix and coarsely grind a combination of grains.

Corn is especially high in carbohydrates and fats, which makes it a good feed for market ducks. But to prevent it from affecting the color and taste of the meat, restrict corn to between 12 and 15 percent of

Nothing makes geese happier than being allowed to graze in a meadow or on a lawn. Make sure any grass you let your geese graze on is free of pesticides and fertilizers to ensure their good health. For more on geese, see page 76.

your market ducks' diet. In the winter months, corn is also good for ornamental ducks that spend some time on the water. Smaller species can eat corn only if it is cracked.

Wheat contains 12.3 percent raw protein; it is the most protein-rich grain. It plays a very important role in the diet of ducks, both as a supplement to other feeds and as a component in commercial mixed feeds. But if ducks eat a diet that contains too much wheat, the protein/carbohydrate balance in their diet may get upset and the food will not be used optimally.

Barley is not very popular with ducks or with other poultry because the grains are pointed and hard; therefore, it is usually coarsely ground and fed in the form of groats. Since barley has a positive effect on meat production as well as on the

quality of the meat, include it in the diet of your market ducks.

Unhulled oats are high in indigestible substances—fiber accounts for as much as 10 percent—and are therefore not as nutrient-rich as other grains, but the roughage is important for proper digestion. Oats have a generally beneficial effect on all kinds of bodily processes, and rolled oats are fed to young chicks of all the members of the poultry family. It has also been asserted that oat hulls in the diet discourage feather eating (see page 55). Oat hulls also result in better breeding results, which is why oats should always be included in the diet of breeding ducks.

Sprouted oats are often given to ducks in the winter months when there is little green food available for them.

Rye, even though most ducks are not fond of it, is an excellent feed grain. Their dislike is based not so much on taste as on the pointed shape of the kernels. To eliminate this problem, feed the birds ground rye in a meal mixture.

Millet is available commercially in several varieties that differ considerably from each other in appearance as well as in nutritional value.

Milo, because of its high protein content, deserves to be singled out. It is a sorghum that comes originally from Africa but is now grown extensively in America. Milo is an excellent feed grain that can be given whole. It is often one of the ingredients in commercial feed mixes.

Spray millet is not recommended for very young ducklings. Because of the hard seed coat, very little of the food value can be absorbed by the digestive system of very young ducks. Hulled millet (which can be quite expensive) can be fed to the ducklings of fancy ornamental breeds.

Middlings are a by-product of grain milling. When flour is produced, the outer cellulose walls of the kernels and bits of the sticky layers underneath are removed. Both the outer cellulose kernel wall and the layers underneath are high in protein, so middlings are a highly valuable animal feed. They are often mixed with boiled potatoes for feeding ducks.

Hemp seed is high in fats and lends gloss to the plumage. It is often given to small ornamental ducks.

No Bread, Please!

Don't feed stale bread to your ducks! Although many of us remember going to the duck pond as children with a bag full of bread crusts to feed the ducks, experts have determined that bread is not healthy for ducks. In some places, it isn't healthy for the environment, either. The state of California has limited access to the Buena Vista Lagoon in Carlsbad (near San Diego) after well-meaning people fed so much bread to the ducks, geese, and swans there that they harmed the lagoon. The birds lost interest in searching for food and started depending on people to feed them. The piles of spoiled bread left by the people attracted rats and pigeons, polluted the water, and became a potential cause of diseases, so the state stepped in and limited access to the duck-feeding area of the lagoon to one day a week in order to maintain the health of the birds and to reduce further damage to the lagoon itself.

Acorns are high in carbohydrates. They are fed whole and unpeeled to dabbling ducks, which are very fond of them.

Potatoes probably play one of the most important roles in the diet of ducks. Ducks like potatoes, which must be cooked and given in combination with proportionate amounts of protein foods since potatoes are almost pure starch. If the potatoes have started sprouting during storage, cut the sprouting eyes out because the shoots contain solanin, which is poisonous. Potatoes are generally combined with meal to form a moist mash of crumbly consistency.

Sugar beets are chopped and steamed for feeding to ducks. Where market ducks are being raised on soft foods, sugar beets are frequently substituted for potatoes.

Carrots are also a nutritious food. Because they are so high in carotene, they are often added to the diet of ducklings. They can be given steamed, chopped, or grated and mixed into the soft food.

Greens are eaten enthusiastically. Nothing will make your utility or ornamental ducks happier than to let them graze on a meadow. Grass does not have much food value, but it does contain vitamins and trace elements, and it provides roughage, which is essential for the digestive process. Feed grass and other greens before they flower because, as the plants age, the proportion of crude fiber in them increases, making them harder to digest. If you give your ducks cut grass, you also have to watch out that the grass stems are not too long. If long stems are swallowed whole, they may compact into balls in the lower, saclike part of the gullet and cause a blockage that may be fatal. Young nettles, dandelions, yarrow, and chickweed are some herbaceous plants that can be chopped fine and added to soft food; ducklings enjoy them in this form.

Duckweeds (*Lemna*), as the name implies, are popular with ducks. These small, free-floating aquatic plants always harbor innumerable small organisms that form an almost indispensable part of the rearing foods for the young of ornamental ducks. Duckweeds have to be very fresh when you give them to ducks. Pour them from a bucket into the ducks' water basin and let the birds sift them out.

If no greens are available for your ducks in the winter, mix some finely chopped lettuce into their food occasionally.

Foods from Animal Sources

Protein from animal sources is absolutely essential in a duck's diet and is available in abundance in many commercial foods.

Blood meal is probably the most protein-rich food. A good brand contains as much as 86 to 89 percent protein. However, blood meal often has acids added to it and, in

Dabbling ducks, such as the northern pintail, forage for food both in the water and on land.

this form, it is not well suited to ducks.

Fish meal is made of whole fish and fish by-products and is manufactured by fish processing plants. It contains proteins that are essential in the diet of ducks. However, the finishing rations given to ducks before slaughter should include meal only from high-quality, low-fat fish, such as cod, that leave no trace of fish smell or taste in the meat. The crucial difference between various fish meals is their fat content, which also determines the price. If the fat content is too high, the fish meal may get rancid if not used soon enough. By the way, none of the good commercial poultry feeds rely exclusively on fish meal for protein; some of the protein is always supplied by meat meal.

Meat meal comes from the meat industry and is made up of meat by-products that are unusable for human consumption. It is a good protein supplement for mixed feeds. There is also a meat meal that comes from the cadavers of domestic animals that have died of natural causes. This meat is processed in accordance with health regulations that ensure that no diseases will be transmitted by it, and it can therefore be used as feed without worry.

Dried shrimp and shrimp meal contain 59 percent protein. These are often mixed into the soft food of ornamental ducks, but they have to be soaked first because they are hard as a rock when dry.

Milk products, with their easily digestible protein, also make good duck food. They can be fed in the

Diving ducks, like the tufted duck, find their food almost exclusively by diving to the bottom of the pond and searching for mussels, clams, snails, or worms.

form of cottage cheese, skim milk, buttermilk, or whey. Fresh cottage cheese—which must, however, be dry—has been successfully used as an easily digestible component in the first food eaten by ducklings (see Feeding Ducklings, page 39). Skim milk and buttermilk are often mixed into the soft food given to ducks raised for market. Feed milk to ducks after it has soured and coagulated. Nonfat powdered milk and dried whey are also good sources of protein and vitamins.

Concentrated protein is a commercially manufactured mixture of animal proteins (fish, blood and meat meals, and powdered milk) and/or vegetable proteins (corn gluten, oil cake, brewer's yeast) that has concentrated vitamins and minerals added to it. To make up for the low-protein content of carbohydrate foods, such as potatoes, add about 15 to 20 percent of a concentrated protein ration to them to achieve the right carbohydrate/protein balance.

Food Supplements

Among these are grit, calcium in the form of phosphate or carbonate of lime, and vitamins.

Grit is a mixture of small grains of quartz and calcareous spar that ducks use to grind down hard food particles in the gizzard (see Digestion, page 29). Ducks need access to this necessary grit at all times.

Phosphate of lime, which is made from bones, is sold commercially as "food lime."

Carbonic lime consists of ground seashells. Female birds have an increased need for calcium during laying season because every new eggshell they manufacture depletes their own bodies of calcium (see Egg Formation and Egg Laying, page 128).

Vitamins are usually present in sufficient quantities in natural ingredients. The commercially available feeds that supply a complete diet (see Complete Rations and Feeds, page 30) also contain all the necessary vitamins in sufficient amounts.

Since commercially available mixes are made up of the ingredients already discussed, it seems appropriate to include them here.

Feed meals, also called dry rations or mash, are mixtures of ingredients designed to meet the nutritional needs of ducks at various times of year and at different stages of life; thus, you can buy commercial rations for ducklings, for young ducks, for laying birds, and for market ducks.

The term "meal" does not imply that the product consists entirely of cereal meals. On the contrary, the feed probably includes ingredients such as blood meal, fish meal, and meat meal, all of which are proteins of animal origin. If such a feed contains all the essential nutrients as established by scientific research, it can be used as the sole food for the ducks.

Where to Buy Duck Feed

Many feed stores carry a varied assortment of feeds suitable for ducks. You can also look for advertisements in poultry magazines to find out what duck feeds are available, or duck breeders will be happy to tell you what their experience with

A Word About Water

Ducks need access to clean, fresh water each day, not just for swimming or bathing, but also for drinking. Because ducks can be particularly susceptible to botulism, a water-borne bacteria, it is up to you, the duck owner, to ensure that the water supply is clean and well aerated because botulism tends to crop up in stale, standing bodies of water during hot, dry weather.

To keep your ducks' water supply clean, remove dead leaves and other organic matter from ponds, and drain and refill the ponds regularly. Also make sure the water supply is free of household chemicals or other pollutants to ensure the health of your birds.

various feeds has been and to give you the names and addresses of their suppliers.

Storing Feeds

• Store grains, pellets, or meals in airtight plastic containers to prevent them from becoming stale or from being eaten by mice or other vermin. Don't store your duck food in galvanized trash cans or other metal containers because metal containers can actually speed up the growth of mold in stored food.

• Keep your duck food in a cool, dry, darkened room because exposure to sunlight or heat can cause the vitamins in the food to break down more rapidly than normal, which means you would be feeding your ducks less nutritious food over time.

• Every couple of weeks, check all the stored feed for signs of vermin. Grain beetles, various moths, mice, and rats can quickly become established if you don't watch out. If your duck food has become moldy, discard it immediately because ducks should never be fed moldy feed. Soft food always has to be fresh; never mix more than your ducks will eat in one day because it spoils quickly in warm weather and then is unfit for consumption.

• Check your food regularly for signs of moisture, mold, or pest infestation. If the food isn't fresh and of top quality, discard it immediately because it's less expensive to replace the food than to treat your flock for illnesses caused by contaminated food.

A duck's bill is a highly specialized tool. Equipped with extremely sensitive tactile organs, it easily detects food and sieves it out of the mud and water.

• Although you may think it's a bargain to purchase a large bag of food, it's probably best to buy smaller bags of food that will stay fresh as you feed your ducks. Check the expiration dates on the food bags, and discard any food left after the expiration date to protect your birds from possible illness.

Feeding

Whether you keep ornamental or utility ducks, you will want to feed them optimally to keep them in the best possible health.

You can either feed your ducks a nutritionally complete ration, or you can feed them a combination of different foods—the choice is up to you. The results of the two feeding methods are the same.

Use plastic or stainless steel dishes to feed your ducks. They are easy to clean and safe to use with either food or water for your birds. Other metals, such as zinc-coated galvanized metals, can leach harmful chemicals into the duck food or water over time and should not be used. Wash bowls daily with hot, soapy water, and rinse them thoroughly before using them again.

Feeding a Complete Ration

The feed industry produces nutritionally complete rations (see page 30) in the form of meals and pellets of various sizes. These rations can be given to the animals without any additional foods. Large-scale duck operations, where tens of thousands of ducks are raised for market, rely entirely on these feeds for economic reasons. If you don't want to mix your ducks' food yourself, you may want to use the commercial rations even though you may have a comparatively small flock.

Many owners of ducks who would rather feed their table scraps and vegetable trimmings to their animals than throw them in the garbage, and who don't mind spending a half hour mixing their ducks' food, will find the second feeding method just right for them.

Feeding a Mixed Diet

To make sure your ducks eat enough of the food you prepare for them, you have to make it appealing and make sure their bills can cope with it. This means that everything is cut to the proper size and that wholesome, but less savory, items are mixed in with the more palatable ones.

When creating your ducks' mixed diet:

- crack grains
- finely chop greens
- cut fruit into pieces
- mash boiled potatoes.

Feed only very fresh greens and grass—on the same day they are cut.

Mix these ingredients together so that the resulting mash is moist but not soggy or runny. It's not as hard to achieve this consistency as it may sound: Just keep stirring liquid (water, skim milk, or whey) into the food until it is moist enough to stick together. If by mistake you add too much liquid and the food gets soupy, just add some dry items.

Don't give your ducks runny foods because it is more difficult for them to pick up with their broad bills than food that is solid enough to stick together. The ducks also get wet food all over their heads and the rest of their feathers, and what gets spilled is stepped on and spread all around the food trough.

Feeding Utility Ducks

Ducks shouldn't eat the same food all the time because their nutritional requirements change with different phases of their life cycle. The body of a fast-growing duckling has different needs than that of a laying duck.

The composition of a diet for utility ducks should be somewhat different for each of the following stages: ducklings, young adult birds, market birds, breeding ducks during laying season, and breeding ducks during the rest period between breeding cycles.

Feeding Ducklings

When ducklings hatch, they have enough food stored in the yolk sac to last them for the first two or three days, which is why they are not fed for the first 24 hours after hatching.

How often to feed: During the first weeks, feed ducklings six or seven times a day at roughly equal intervals. Reduce the number of meals to between three and five in the course of the second to the eighth week. During weeks eight to twelve, three meals are sufficient.

How much to feed: It is difficult to say just how much food a duckling consumes a day because some ducklings are very active eaters, while others are extremely modest in their food consumption. But even beginners have no problem telling how much they should give their ducklings to eat. When all the food is eaten between meals, it is time to increase the ration. Keep increasing the amount until some food is left over, which is a clear sign that the birds have had enough to eat. Breeders sometimes call this "feeding to satiation."

During the first three weeks, feed the ducklings exclusively on a nutritionally complete commercial duckling ration that contains 18 percent protein and is made up of pellets ⅛ inch (3 mm) in diameter. Place a shallow dish with drinking water next to the feeder.

If you don't want to feed your ducks a commercial ration, you can compose your own: Combine 40 parts oat flakes, 40 parts cracked barley for chicks, 20 parts bran, and some finely chopped greens, and add water while stirring constantly until the mixture is moist but still crumbly. Feed this food to the ducklings from the first through the seventh day. From the eighth through the twenty-seventh day, feed a soft food made of 60 parts cracked cereals (corn, oats, barley), 15 parts protein foods (soured milk or cottage cheese), and 25 parts greens. From the fourth week on, you can give them a mixture of 25 parts boiled and mashed potatoes, 35 parts cracked cereals, 15 parts protein foods, and 25 parts greens.

In addition to the mixed foods, the ducklings should have grit and calcium (see page 36) in separate dishes.

Feeding Market Ducks

Rations for market ducks are designed to produce the greatest weight gain within the shortest period of time while using as little feed as possible. In the method that is now used universally to produce market ducklings—which attain a weight of 5½ pounds (2.5 kg) by the time they are eight or nine weeks old—the birds eat rations for fast growth from the day they are hatched. During the first eight or nine weeks, the ducklings multiply their hatching weight by 50 at an average consumption of feed of 20 to 22 pounds (9 to 10 kg). It is hardly surprising that such dramatic growth requires a diet high in protein. Using a commercial, nutritionally complete ration takes the least amount of effort and reduces waste of food to a minimum.

Complete ration for ducklings: During their first three weeks of life, ducklings raised for market receive a ration with an 18 percent protein content and a pellet size of ⅛ inch (2.5 mm).

Complete ration for market ducks: From the fourth week on, the birds are given a ration with 16 percent protein and a pellet size of ³⁄₁₆ inch (4.5 mm), and this diet is maintained until the ducks are ready for slaughter at eight or nine weeks.

Both of these feeds are also available in the form of meals or mash.

Fattening ducks on potatoes: On some farms, potatoes are still used to fatten ducks. The potatoes, which contain very little protein, have to be fortified with a mixture of cracked grains and a protein concentrate (see page 36). For best weight gain, a proportion of 65 percent mashed potatoes to 35 percent mixed protein food is recommended. Ducks readily eat this food, and it can be made even more appealing by adding some skim milk. It is given three times a day in sufficient amounts so that after the ducks have eaten their fill, there is still a little left over for the next few hours—however, the food should all be gone by the next scheduled feeding.

The total amount eaten during nine weeks of feeding is about 33 to 44 pounds (15 to 20 kg) of potatoes and about 11 pounds (5 kg) of mixed protein food per bird.

Note: Ducklings raised for market are not provided with a swimming basin, but they need to be able to take baths several times a week.

Feeding Laying Ducks

Ducklings destined to be layers are fed on the same regimen for the first seven weeks as those raised for market. From the eighth through the thirteenth week, the time when they undergo the juvenile molt, the future laying ducks need a 14 percent protein diet. A nutritionally complete ration for young hens that has a protein content of 14 percent is generally used for this period.

Utility ducks become sexually active when they are five to seven months old. Lightweight breeds, such as runners and Campbells, start laying eggs as early as five to six months; heavyweight types such as the Pekin, Aylesbury, and Rouen ducks mature later and don't start laying until seven months.

Single ration: About two to four weeks before the ducks are expected to start laying, they are shifted over to a ration for breeding birds. The simplest method is to give them a nutritionally complete, 16 percent protein ration for laying hens.

Mixed food: If no appropriate commercial ration is available, laying ducks can be given 80 percent cracked grains and 20 percent meat or fish meal.

If you want to use potatoes for your laying ducks, combine 25 percent mashed potatoes, 10 percent cracked corn, 10 percent cracked rye, 10 percent wheat middlings, 10 percent fish meal, 10 percent meat meal, and 25 percent mixed grains composed of corn, oats, and barley.

Another alternative is to compose a feed of 70 percent potatoes, 8 percent chopped sugar beets, 7 percent wheat middlings, 5 percent cracked corn and oats, and 10 percent meat meal.

Feeding During the Rest Period

When the breeding ducks stop laying, which is usually in the fall, they receive a "maintenance" diet. This diet contains fewer calories than the laying mash the birds have been eating because their hormonal activities should slow down until the next laying season starts. If you kept on feeding the birds a laying diet, they would continue producing eggs (though at longer intervals) until physically exhausted. The maintenance diet is supposed to keep the birds in good condition without letting them get fat or stimulating any sexual drives. For this purpose, a nutritionally complete, 14-percent-protein ration for young hens has been used with good results.

Feeding Ornamental Ducks

There are no special, nutritionally complete rations on the market for ornamental ducks. These birds are given the same kinds of food as utility ducks, without the rations for raising market ducks. Trying to adjust the feed to the age of the birds and to the seasons works only if you keep your ducks in an aviary or on a small backyard pond. If they live in larger enclosures or on more extensive bodies of water, attempts to control their diet are pointless.

Most people who keep ducks in such a setting have more than one species, and the birds are of different ages and follow different breeding calendars. Wild birds will show up at the feeding stations and will consume a considerable share of your duck food. You will have to put out food several times a day to ensure that your ornamental birds do not go hungry. Under such conditions, all you can do is supply an adequate all-purpose diet all year. But if you keep ornamental ducks in an aviary or on a pond in an enclo-sure in your backyard, I recommend the following:

Ducklings: Feed a nutritionally complete ration in the form of a mash containing 16 percent protein for the first three weeks. In the first week, to get them interested in eating, add finely chopped, hard-boiled egg yolk and enough water for the feed to be moist but still crumbly. Sprinkle finely chopped greens over the top and, if possible, put a shallow dish full of water and duckweed next to the mixed food.

Feed the ducklings six or seven times a day at regular intervals for the first two weeks. Feed them to satiation, that is, just as much as they will consume at feeding time. Always remove the leftovers because they spoil quickly.

When the ducklings are three weeks old, they can start eating small seeds such as silver millet, birdseed mixtures for canaries and/or parakeets, and finely cracked wheat, in addition to the ration they have been receiving. Sprinkle the seeds into a shallow dish with water, where the ducklings will gobble them up. Be sure to always have sand and grit available.

Starting with the fourth or fifth week, gradually shift the ducklings from a diet for ducklings to one for adult birds. Make this transition by mixing a little more of the new food into the accustomed fare every day.

Mature birds: I recommend using soft food made up of 30 percent mashed potatoes, 10 percent wheat middlings, 20 percent cracked barley, 20 percent chopped dry shrimp,

If you have a large lawn or pasture on your property, let your domestic ducks loose on it. Many breeds of duck will wander around like sheep, cropping young grass and tender leaves.

15 percent bread, and 5 percent crushed seashells. Add whatever greens are in season, finely chopped.

Laying birds: In an aviary or on a garden pond, I recommend a nutritionally complete, 16-percent-protein pelleted ration for laying hens. Start giving it one month before the laying season of the particular species of ornamental or wild duck that you have begins.

During the *rest period*, give ornamental ducks a nutritionally complete, 14-percent-protein ration designed for young hens.

A Duck Pasture

If you have a fairly large area of lawn or meadow, let your domestic ducks loose on it. They will busily comb the area for snails, slugs, caterpillars, and worms. They keep the grass down at the same time, and are especially fond of the tender, small leaves of plants. Ducks like nettle shoots, dandelion greens, yarrow, orache, chicory, and chickweed. After the ducks have finished grazing, the grass will grow back healthy and dark green; the ducks have not only kept the grass short but also fertilized the lawn.

If you let your ducks graze, make sure they are grazing on pesticide-free grass to protect them from accidental poisoning and keep them away from potentially poisonous plants, such as oleander. In the evening, offer your ducks a handful of grain each in their quarters.

Chapter Five

Care and Maintenance

Quarantine

It would be a serious mistake to place newly acquired ducks in a yard where other waterfowl are already living. First of all, there is the possibility that the newcomers, which are still unsure of themselves and timid, would be persecuted and possibly killed by the already established birds. But there is an even greater danger: The new birds might introduce a disease into a previously healthy flock. That is why new birds have to be quarantined for at least a month or, if there is any reason to be suspicious, longer. This means that you have to have a separate space, apart from the main duck yard, to house new birds for an observation period, and that you have to feed and water the quarantined ducks separate from your main flock with different food and water containers. You will also have to disinfect your shoes, feeding utensils, and hands to reduce the chance of transmitting disease from the quarantined birds to your main flock. Wash your hands and utensils carefully with hot, soapy water, rinse thoroughly, and set up disinfectant shoe baths outside the quarantine area.

Proper Acclimation

If your new ducks pass quarantine with flying colors and you want to let them join the other occupants of the pond, watch them for some time to see how the already established flock reacts to the newcomers. Don't remain standing right next to the pond, however, because your presence will distract all the birds. Watch from a distance to check if the encounter is peaceful or if it gives rise to fighting.

To ensure the greatest chance of a successful introduction, bring new birds into your flock at the right time of year. The information below will give you some ideas of the best times of year to introduce new ducks, as well as some of the environmental considerations they require.

Fall or winter: These are the best seasons for unfamiliar ducks to get used to each other. At this time, older birds are most likely to put up with newcomers because their hormonal activity is at a low ebb (see The Reproductive Period, page 86) and the birds are consequently less aggressive. In the wild, too, many species of ducks live together peacefully during the winter.

By the time the courtship period starts in the spring, all the ducks are so used to each other that serious conflicts are rare. If you house your ducks on a large enough pond so that the birds have enough room to get away from each other if necessary, the ducks described in this book are very unlikely to fight.

Ducks that live in aviaries or small garden ponds, however, see each other constantly, and this triggers territorial behavior from pairs that are ready to breed. This aggressive defense of territory is one of the main reasons why you should limit the number of ducks you keep in a given space.

Food intake: After you've introduced new ducks, check that the new birds are really eating. Sometimes established birds don't let the new ones near the feeding stations. Because ducks can live without food for a long time (up to two weeks), the fact that your ducks are still alive after one week does not mean that they have been eating regularly. To be on the safe side, set up several feeding stations located at some distance from each other. This arrangement should permit the newcomers to get sufficient food.

Cover: Make sure the yard offers enough cover so that ducks that are pursued by aggressive birds can find hiding places. The saying "out of sight, out of mind" aptly describes the behavior of birds. When the pursuer no longer can see its victim, the chase usually ends.

Tameness: If your new ducks are very timid, you should always move quietly in their yard. Ducks—both ornamental and utility breeds—are naturally apprehensive and always ready to take off in flight, and they do not tame as easily as geese. This is one reason why duck farms that raise market ducks try to avoid changes in the personnel in charge of the birds and why visitors are not allowed in the duck buildings. The birds would get so excited and upset that it might interfere with their putting on weight. Ornamental ducks don't become as friendly toward their keepers as geese do, either, but in time your birds may build up sufficient confidence and trust to take food from your hand.

Keeping Ducks in an Aviary

Certain species of ornamental ducks are kept almost exclusively in aviaries, which offer certain advantages over an open pond, including:

• Protection from predators for small and very valuable ornamental species.

• Steady access to food, as opposed to competition from wild ducks landing on an open pond.

• The ability to control breeding, which is a factor with certain species,

Keeping ducks on a pond allows the duck keeper to enjoy the birds in a more natural habitat, but it also poses some potential risks to the birds from predators.

such as the red-crested pochard, the rosy-bill, the spotbill duck, the cinnamon teal, and the blue-winged teal, which commonly crossbreed when they are kept together.

Keeping Ducks on a Pond

Keeping ducks on a pond allows you to watch them without the visual interference of wire mesh. By planting the surroundings of the pond imaginatively (see Planting the Pond and Its Surroundings, page 17), you can create miniature landscapes that often closely resemble the ducks' natural habitat. The great drawback to the pond setting is that predators, both on the ground and from the air, have easy access to the ducks, their eggs, and the ducklings. Also, wild ducks may drop in uninvited, which can lead to greater food consumption and consequently

increased costs. And, as mentioned above, crossbreeding is almost inevitable if you keep several related species together. Since male hybrids never have the same brightness of plumage as normal males of

Predators to Consider

You need to consider the safety of your ducks as you set up feeding and sleeping areas for them on your property. Here are some predators to be aware of:

From the air: Hawks, owls, crows, and magpies

From the water: Snapping turtles and large fish

From the ground: Coyotes, snakes, raccoons, opossums, foxes, martens, mink, weasels, and domestic dogs and cats

Take appropriate steps to ensure the safety of your ducks by providing them as safe a living space as possible.

the species, they cannot be sold to fanciers and, therefore, usually end up in the soup pot.

In other parts of the world, such as China and some parts of eastern Europe, utility ducks—almost always Pekin ducks—are quite often kept and raised for market on large ponds. Raising ducks by this method is relatively cheap because the ducks forage for most of their food and receive only supplementary feedings. Whether ducks can reach their optimal weight under this system is, however, questionable and obviously depends on how plentiful the food is in a particular body of water.

Keeping Ducks Indoors

Ornamental as well as utility ducks are kept indoors primarily to keep them out of the winter cold and secondarily to protect them against predators. When their pond freezes, the ducks move into their winter quarters. Be sure to move tropical species indoors before the first freeze because ornamental ducks that are native to the tropics and muscovy ducks can easily freeze their toes and webs if they are out in the snow and ice.

Commercial ducks are locked in their houses at night year-round to keep them safe from martens, foxes, cats, and dogs. During the day, they are usually let out into runs that are enclosed with fences 16 inches (40 cm) high. Only ducks raised for market are kept indoors all the time to avoid a slowing of weight gain because of too much physical activity.

Ducks as Pets

Although it may strike some as a strange concept, the idea of keeping ducks as pets is catching on in North America. From children who want to keep their 4-H project bird as a pet to adults who are captivated by the charm and personality of different breeds, pet ducks are being kept and appreciated for being pets, rather than their usefulness as a producer of eggs, feathers, or meat.

To be successful as a pet duck owner, it's important to do your research ahead of time to learn the pros and cons of keeping a duck as a pet. Among the pros are the cuddly nature of some birds, as well as their curiosity and entertaining antics. Some ducks have learned to do tricks, while others are content to be held on their owners' laps or sit near them for cuddling.

One of the major cons to keeping ducks as pets is their elimination habits. Ducks are unable to be potty-trained because they lack the sphincter muscle needed to control their elimination. To overcome this obstacle, several companies have created special duck diapers that allow ducks to be kept as indoor pets.

Trick-Training a Duck

With patience and short practice sessions every day, you may be able to train your duck to come when called or to perform other simple tricks. The key to success is short daily practice sessions (about 10 minutes maximum) and to stop training your duck while the training session is fun for both of you.

Duck Projects for Children and Teens

Children in 4-H or teens in FFA can raise ducks as project animals. These projects teach important skills, such as animal care, budgeting, and showmanship, as well as providing tangible rewards, such as ribbons or other prizes. In addition to raising ducks, children and teens can use ducks to study embryology, wildlife management, and habitat restoration with these organizations.

In addition to raising ducks as project animals in 4-H or FFA, Boy or Girl Scout troops can build and install duck houses or nest boxes in wetland areas near you as service projects. Setting up a duck pond or other habitat can also help a Boy Scout earn his Bird Study merit badge or help a Girl Scout earn her All About Birds interest project award. Camp Fire members can also earn Nature Lore honor beads by raising ducks or other poultry at home.

Letting Ducks Roam

Utility Ducks

If you have a meadow or a field for grazing livestock, with or without a body of water, turn your ducks loose on it (see A Duck Pasture, page 43). You don't need to worry that your ducks might fly off because most commercial ducks are no longer capable of taking to the air. If you have a breed that can still fly, such as muscovies or call ducks, you still have no reason for concern. If you offer them some food every evening, such as a handful of grain per bird, the birds will return punctually to their shelter to get it. Earthbound ducks such as Pekins, Rouens, Aylesburys, and runners will come, too, waddling as fast as their feet will carry them to the feeders to get their evening treat.

Ornamental Ducks

Letting ornamental ducks run free on unfenced land is not a good idea. Flightless birds can wander far afield, get lost, and become easy prey for predators. With ornamental ducks, you must remember that you are dealing with wild animals that have, at best, a very tenuous bond to humans.

Some nature lovers wonder why the ponds in our parks are populated primarily by swans and why some equally beautiful ornamental ducks are not to be found there. The

Questions for Pet Duck Owners

Do you have time for a pet duck? Pet ducks require more one-on-one time from their owners than do ducks that live in flocks on a backyard pond. Backyard ducks need daily attention for feeding and maintenance, while pet ducks look to their owners to be their "flock."

Do you have space for a pet duck? Pet ducks need a safe, enclosed area in which they can rest or sleep, as well as a place to swim or bathe. They must also be supervised indoors to ensure that they do not cause harm to themselves by eating something harmful or becoming entangled in power cords or mini-blind cords, or otherwise injure themselves.

Do you have the money for a pet duck? Pet ducks need food, water, and regular veterinary care. They may also end up in situations in which emergency medical care is required. Make sure you can afford a duck before you bring one home.

Will you be interested in your duck in 5, 10, or 20 years? Ideally, any pet ownership situation is for the life of the pet. Pet ducks can live up to 20 years, depending on the breed, and it would be cruel to bring a duck into your home and then lose interest in it in a few years.

Are there other pets already in your home? Ducks can be integrated into a home with other pets, but caution and common sense should be the key to introducing your duck to existing pets. Large dogs may want to hunt your duck if it is an adult, or your cat may think a duckling is a new form of play toy. If you have large lizards or other reptiles in your home, they may simply view the duck as dinner and attempt to eat it if the duck is left unsupervised near the reptile.

reason is primarily practical: The ducks would have to share their food with many wild birds and would have to be fed four or five times a day. The money budgeted by park administrators for feeding wildlife is rather modest in most cases and doesn't usually permit the purchase of food in the required amounts.

Turn ducks loose in your garden or backyard only if your flowerbeds and the vegetable patch are fenced and out of reach of ever-hungry duck bills. Your ornamental duck area, which should include a pond and some dry land, has to be fenced, too, and it should take in as much grassy area as is feasible.

Regular Handling Helps Build Trust

Ducks begin to develop trust in their owners through regular, gentle handling, so duck owners who want their ducks to be more pet-like should handle the birds every day.

Since ducks crop the grass quite close to the ground, you can usually replace your lawn mower with this truly organic system of lawn care.

Rendering Ducks Flightless or Letting Them Fly Freely

All ornamental ducks are fast, agile flyers, while only a few breeds of commercial ducks have retained their ability to fly. Among these are the call duck, the East Indie, and the muscovy duck. The other breeds, including Pekin, Aylesbury, and Rouen ducks, are much too heavy to fly or, like the runner, have changed so much in body shape as a result of selective breeding that they couldn't get airborne no matter how hard they tried.

Anyone who has flighted ducks and lets them roam freely must be especially careful that they don't take off for good some day. With large collections of ornamental ducks, it is not uncommon for some young ducks to disappear when they have learned to fly.

Rendering ducks flightless: One can keep birds from flying either temporarily or permanently. In the temporary method, you trim the primary feathers of one wing with scissors. The permanent method, which is best done when a duckling is two or three days old, consists of pinion-ing or removing a few small bones that support the wing on one side.

Note: In some countries, wing pinioning is subject to animal welfare legislation, and in many regions only veterinarians are allowed to perform the operation. You should check with your veterinarian or with appropriate authorities to find out if there are any laws of this kind in effect in your state or province.

When you trim the feathers of one wing, they will grow in after the next molt (see page 85), and the duck will once again be able to fly. You therefore have to watch every year when the birds molt and catch them for wing clipping just before they regain their flying power. Ask someone who has done it before to show you how to trim the wings properly.

Flying freely: Utility breeds such as the muscovy are often allowed to fly as they wish on farms. These birds find most of their own food in the surrounding area and always return home in the evening to get their daily ration. However, this method is not recommended for

Don't Free Your Duck in the Wild

Although you may think your ornamental or utility duck can fare well in the wild, you may be wrong. Ducks that have become accustomed to being cared for by people lose their survival skills, and they will quickly perish if they are turned loose in the wild.

Rouen and Pekin ducks are among the breeds of commercial ducks that have lost the ability to fly as they have developed into utility breeds.

someone living in a suburb. The unrestrained ducks would be sure to plunder all your neighbors' gardens, which would make you highly unpopular.

Daily Chores

When you make your morning rounds to ensure that all is well in your duck area, the first thing to do is to make sure that all birds are still present and that none of them is sick. Small ornamental ducks often hide in shrubbery. If they don't make an appearance when you put down food, you should start looking for them. If females of an ornamental species suddenly disappear in the spring, this often means that they have built a nest in some hidden spot and are brooding.

After cleaning the feeders, put out only enough food to last the ducks until evening (see Feeding Ornamental Ducks, page 42). In an unenclosed yard, food quickly attracts rats and mice. If the ducks have to stay indoors because of severe cold, replace the drinking and bathing water frequently. Change wet bedding or cover it with a layer of dry litter.

As you clean your duck yard or shelter, it's a good idea to wear rubber gloves. Some ducks can carry salmonella or other diseases that can be transmitted to people, so rubber

Because small natural ponds can be difficult to keep clean, it's best to keep only a few ducks on them.

leaves, twigs, and hunks of dirt—anything that could plug up the drain—that may be floating on the surface. After removing all the debris, unscrew the overflow pipe from the drainpipe and let the water drain out.

When all the water is gone, shovel out the mud that has settled on the bottom. If the walls of the pond are dirty and covered with algae, scrub them with a coarse broom or brush and regular tap water. Once all the dirt is gone, disinfect the pond walls with a chlorine solution, which can be purchased at a garden center. Follow the directions on the package for proper dilution. After letting the chlorine work for half an hour, rinse it carefully off the walls with a garden hose. Wait until the rinse water is also completely drained out. Then screw the overflow pipe back into the drainpipe, and fill the pond with fresh water.

Follow the same procedure for cleaning a pond in an aviary. This is easier because aviary ponds are usually smaller than garden ponds.

Cleaning a Natural Pond

Small natural ponds or small craters that have filled with ground water are difficult to keep clean. The most you can do is to remove dead fish and various other trash with a rake. Because these bodies of water are so difficult to clean, keep only a very few ducks on such a pond in order not to disturb the biological self-cleaning action of the natural body of water. If the water starts getting dirty, keep the ducks away (see

gloves are recommended to protect you from contracting a disease. If you don't wear rubber gloves, be sure to wash your hands with hot, soapy water after you handle your ducks or their waste, and don't let children play with the ducks unsupervised because they may put their unwashed hands or fingers into their mouths after handling the ducks.

Sanitary Measures

How to Change the Pond Water

The water in your garden pond should not stand long enough to turn into a muddy, foul-smelling brew. How often you change your pond water depends on the number of ducks you keep on it. Before changing the water, collect all the feathers,

Goldeneyes breed only on ponds with clean, clear water.

Botulism, page 58). Larger ponds with reed and rush growth along the edges are usually self-cleaning.

Cleaning a Duck House

Duck houses, where birds destined for market are housed, get dirty very quickly. This is why sanitation is especially important here. Whenever the litter gets wet, remove it or cover it with layers of dry straw. Simply covering up the soaked litter is a perfectly sanitary way of dealing with it as long as the flock is healthy. In the runs of ornamental or utility ducks, remove droppings that have been walked on and mashed into the ground with a spade. Scrub feeders and water dishes daily with a coarse brush.

Whitewash: Whitewashing the walls of the duck house once a year is part of keeping the place hygienic. The lime in the whitewashed solution has only minimal disinfecting power, but the solution can be made more potent by adding 4 ounces of Lysol per gallon (118 ml per 3.78 L) or 6 ounces of Clorox per gallon (177 ml per 3.78 L).

To make an effective whitewash, mix 10 quarts (10 L) of regular whitewash with ¼ pound (125 gm) potato starch, a handful of cooking salt, and 10 ounces (295 ml) of Lysol. Apply whitewash solutions immediately after mixing.

Cleaning an Aviary

In an aviary, collect and remove all the droppings on the ground every day, and clean the water basin daily. When the breeding season is over, take out the nest boxes and other nest sites, and discard any nesting materials. Disinfect the inside walls of the nest boxes with a chlorine solution, then stack and store the nest boxes until the next breeding season.

Chapter Six

Health Care and Diseases

Preventive Care

Compared to other bird families, properly cared-for ornamental or commercial ducks are subject to relatively few diseases. Preventive care is of special importance, however, and it is essential that you observe the following basic rules:

• Because many infections are transmitted through excreta, keep the shelters, yards, and swimming water clean.

This is what a healthy male mallard looks like. He stands upright and pays attention to his surroundings. His eyes are bright and his plumage is well maintained. In contrast, a sick one will lie on the ground for long periods of time with closed eyes. Its plumage will be in disarray, and it will produce frequent, runny droppings.

• A good, nutritious diet even during the winter months makes ducks more resistant to disease and helps prevent metabolic and deficiency diseases (see Feeding, page 38).

• Newly acquired ducks must be kept separate from the established birds for at least a month because they might otherwise introduce pathogens into your flock (see Quarantine, page 44).

• New ducks need time to adjust to their new situation so that they can defend themselves adequately against the established birds (see Proper Acclimation, page 44).

If a Duck Gets Sick

If you watch your birds regularly, changes in their behavior will become obvious to you very quickly (see table, page 56). A duck is sick if:

• It lies on the ground for unusually long periods of time and is reluctant to enter the water.

• Its breast and abdominal feathers lack luster and look stringy.

• Its natural escape reactions are slow or lacking altogether.

- It has very little or no interest in food.
- Its breastbone protrudes sharply (you can check this by feeling the breast area with your hand).
- A drake fails to grow his usual nuptial plumage in the fall.

Externally Visible Problems

Lameness

Cause: Lameness is quite common in ducks. If the birds are kept on a hard floor, whether it is tile or packed dirt, their sensitive toes and webs suffer. The soles and the balls of the feet are compacted, which sooner or later leads to calluses. In many cases, pus forms underneath the callous layer of the skin and gradually hardens into a cheeselike mass.

Signs: To try to minimize the pain in their feet, the ducks often lie around on land and limp into the water when people approach.

Treatment: Treating this kind of condition is difficult and a cure is far from assured. Take the affected duck to a veterinarian, who will remove the calluses and scrape out as much of the pus as possible. The duck's foot is then bandaged, and the duck should be placed on a soft surface, such as sawdust, peat moss, or rubber mats.

Prevention: Try not to have large, hard areas in the duckyard. Cover concrete floors with sand, for instance, and spade and hoe packed dirt frequently.

Slipped Wing or Angel Wing

Cause: This condition is the result of weak tendons in young birds, but it is not hereditary. In utility ducks raised for market, slipped wings are no serious matter, but in breeding stock and in ornamental ducks, a slipped wing is a real flaw. Young muscovy ducks are especially prone to this condition.

Signs: The distal joints of the wings with the heavy quills (the developing primary feathers) get very heavy in growing birds and are sometimes so weighty that they twist outward and downward. As a consequence, one or both wings stick out of from the body at almost a right angle.

Treatment: In its early stages, this condition can be cured. The veterinarian places the wing in its normal position, inserts a wad of cotton between the body and the wing, and tapes everything in place with an adhesive bandage. In addition, the duckling is wrapped in a cotton or linen bandage that passes both in front of and in back of the legs and across the back. After two weeks, the bandages can be removed, and the wing will stay in its normal position.

Feather Plucking and Feather Eating

Cause: Several reasons may be behind this habit, but it is not entirely clear what roles they all play. Feather plucking and feather eating

Important Signs of Illness

Signs	Possible Causes
Drab-looking, dry plumage	Improper diet or environmental conditions; in artificially brooded chicks, stress and insufficient secretion from the oil gland
Wing hanging down almost vertically in young ducks	Slipped wing
Feather eating and feather plucking in young ducks	Boredom, particularly in market ducks raised in overcrowded conditions
Incomplete molting of drakes from eclipse to nuptial plumage	Internal disease, metabolic problem, sign of old age
Bare places on the back of head and on neck of females	Fights with other ducks, the drake grabbing her by the head feathers in the course of mating
Withering and loss of toes and webs in tropical ducks	Freezing in ice-cold water if kept on pond during winter

*If the following signs are observed, consult a veterinarian immediately.

Pumping breathing with open bill	Aspergillosis or possibly salmonellosis
Retching motions of neck and head and rapid weight loss in ducklings three or more weeks old	Infestation with gizzard worms
Lying on the ground with outstretched neck and signs of paralysis	Botulism poisoning
Loss of balance, reeling	First signs of botulism poisoning, salmonellosis, or viral hepatitis
Listlessness, falling over and lying on the side, convulsive listless paddling motions of the feet—in ducklings two or three weeks old	Viral hepatitis
Apathy and ruffled feathers in females, often sitting in "penguin stance," sticky plumage in caudal region	Egg binding
Plumage in caudal region smeared with runny droppings of various colors	Enteritis as a result of improper diet, poisoning, or salmonellosis
Limping	Cornlike calluses and sores on the bottoms of the pads and joints of the feet; also seen with salmonellosis

are common in mass operations where many ducks are confined in small areas. The problem is especially prevalent in immature ducks at the time they lose their down and the adult plumage grows in (see The Molt, page 85).

Signs: Usually the drakes that are most advanced in development start plucking and eating the blood-filled quills of other ducklings. First, they bite off the feathers on their fellows' backs, then move on to the wings and to other parts of the body.

Treatment: A number of methods to try to stop feather eating have been tried, such as increasing the protein content in the ducks' diet and changing the lighting in the duck houses—without significant results so far.

Dry Plumage

Cause: Ducklings that hatch under a broody hen or in an artificial incubator have little or no oil on their down plumage. When a mother duck broods her ducklings, their down plumage becomes water-repellent through contact with her plumage. Ducklings hatch with the innate ability to grease their feathers with the secretions of their uropygial or oil glands, but during the first few days the glands do not produce enough oil to waterproof the plumage effectively.

Signs: Ducklings incubated by broody hens or in artificial incubators drown when they try to swim because their dry feathers get waterlogged.

Treatment: If you should witness such an incident, quickly grab the duckling, rub its feathers dry, and set it under a heat lamp.

Prevention: Keep all ducklings—both ornamental and utility breeds—that were not brooded by ducks away from water at first. Then introduce them to water gradually by setting up shallow basins. Their uropygial glands will soon start secreting oil so that the ducklings can grease their feathers themselves. Many breeders of ornamental and commercial ducks who want to avoid all risk don't let their ducklings near water until the down on their breasts and abdomens has been replaced by permanent feathers.

Internal Diseases

Salmonellosis

Cause: Bacteria of the genus *Salmonella* are the causative agents of this disease, which can spread like an epidemic and cause huge losses where ducks are raised on a large scale. The immediate cause of an outbreak may be dirty eggshells, insufficiently disinfected incubators or rearing boxes, or generally unsanitary conditions in the brooder house. Some laying ducks constantly eliminate salmonella bacteria in their excreta, or the droppings of a single sick duckling may spread the disease quickly throughout the entire flock. Since ornamental ducks are rarely kept or raised in large numbers, the disease is uncommon among them.

Note: Salmonellosis is transmissible to humans. If you have people with compromised immune systems (such as cancer patients undergoing chemotherapy) or small children in your household, keep them away from duck droppings.

Signs: Ducks suffering from salmonellosis often show no clear clinical signs. The most common signs are diarrhea and lameness caused by swollen joints and paralysis. Sick ducklings often sit in groups under a heat lamp with raised feathers and half-closed eyes. Death may follow quickly or not until after several days of sickness. Birds that survive the sickness harbor the dangerous bacteria and pass them on in their droppings and their eggs for the rest of their lives. If you can identify the carrier birds in your flock, it is best to remove them to prevent further spread of the disease.

Treatment: An absolute diagnosis of salmonellosis is possible only through a bacteriological analysis of the droppings or the organs of deceased birds. If you suspect the disease, send droppings and cadavers to a veterinary laboratory as quickly as possible. Antibiotics can be effective against this disease.

Botulism (Limberneck)

Cause: In the late summer and early fall, mass dying is sometimes caused by the bacterium *Clostridium botulinum* among ducks and other waterfowl on park waters. The disease tends to occur in bodies of water without outlets and in still bays of lakes during dry summers with lots of sunshine. In the warm oxygen-deficient waters, botulism bacteria multiply rapidly in mud and decaying animal matter. The ducks get sick from ingesting decaying vegetable and animal matter and maggots containing the toxin produced by the bacteria, a toxin that is one of the most deadly organic nerve poisons in existence.

The strain of botulism that most commonly affects ducks does not seem to infect humans, so there is no danger of the disease spreading to humans who touch sick or dead ducks, their droppings, or the contaminated water and mud in a duck pond.

Signs: Depending on the amount and concentration of the toxin absorbed, the ducks may die within a few hours without any previous signs of illness, or lie on the shore, paralyzed but conscious, with half-closed eyes and straight necks because they have lost control of their neck muscles.

Treatment: If the disease is caught early, treatment may be possible, although most severely ill birds die within 24 to 48 hours. Affected birds should receive fluids, force-feedings until they can eat on their own, and be kept in a cool environment. Antitoxin may also be useful in treating botulism in ducks. Consult your veterinarian for more information.

Prevention: Keep healthy ducks away from contaminated waters. In a small natural pond, you can search the bottom with nets for dead animals and pipe fresh water into the pond. This deprives the botulism bacteria of the medium in which they thrive. A botulism vaccine for ducks is under development in Japan.

Infectious Hepatitis (Viral Hepatitis)

Cause: This form of hepatitis is caused by a virus and accounts for great losses among ducklings two to three weeks old. The virus is ingested in food and droppings, and it is also absorbed from the air. It is not communicable to humans.

Signs: Affected ducklings suffer from disturbed equilibrium, lie on their sides, have their heads drawn back toward their tails, and make convulsive paddling motions with their legs. The sickness often lasts no more than one day and generally ends in death. At necropsy, the liver is conspicuously enlarged, yellow, and full of dotlike hemorrhages.

Treatment: If there is an outbreak of viral hepatitis in a flock, vaccination can save ducklings that are still healthy. Birds that recover from the virus are considered immune.

Prevention: Vaccinating breeding ducks two weeks to a month before egg laying is recommended because the mother's immunity is passed through the egg to the offspring.

Aspergillosis (Brooder Pneumonia)

Cause: The causative agent, a fungus of the *Aspergillus* genus, is found worldwide and especially affects very young ducklings. It can

This duckling seems to have a healthy, normal appetite, but a sick duckling may be unwilling to eat. Other signs of illness in ducks can include fluffed feathers, listlessness, or a willingness to sleep more than normal. Take note of your birds' routine so you will know what is normal for them.

also sometimes affect mature ducks. The fungus forms a grayish green to blackish mold on damp feed, dirty litter, and decaying organic material of all kinds. The spores become airborne at the slightest air movement and are then inhaled by the ducks. In healthy birds, the spores remain inactive, but in ducks with lowered resistance as a result of improper environmental conditions, they propagate. In such birds, a solid lining of fungi forms on the moist inside walls of the respiratory organs, leading to clogging of narrow passages, such as the bronchia. The fungi also produce highly toxic waste substances that affect the bird's entire body.

Signs: Affected birds gasp for breath while opening and shutting their bills rhythmically. Eventually, they suffocate.

Treatment: Diagnosis and treatment can be difficult.

Prevention: The best precaution to take against this disease is to disinfect the housing and the incubating rooms regularly. Disinfect incubators both before the eggs are placed in them and after the ducklings hatch. Remove damp litter, droppings, and all spilled food as promptly as possible.

Roundworms

Cause: Roundworms are parasites from the *Ascaridia* genus that are picked up by ducks from the soil in their duck yards or by ingesting an insect or other animal that carries a roundworm inside it. Once the roundworm enters the duck's body, it can lay its eggs in the bird's digestive tract. Large-scale infestations can block the duck's digestive tract or weaken the bird's immune system so a secondary infection sets in.

Signs: Young birds are most likely to be infected. Their wings droop and they sit listlessly with their feathers ruffled. They do not grow and develop well, and they have loose droppings.

Treatment: Your veterinarian can prescribe a deworming medication to rid your duck of roundworms.

Prevention: Roundworms do not thrive in clean, well-maintained surroundings, so protect your birds from infection by keeping their food and water bowls scrupulously clean. Routinely test and treat younger birds to help maintain flock health.

Gizzard Worms

Cause: The *Echinuria* worm is transmitted to ducks by way of water fleas. These tiny crustaceans ingest the worm eggs in their food, and the eggs develop into larvae in a few days. If water fleas with worm larvae find their way into a duck's stomach, the parasites burrow deep into the stomach lining. There they form cysts the size of a lentil or a pea that protrude and often densely cover an area. These protruberances can block the narrow passage between the proventriculus and the gizzard and thus keep the food from moving on. The blockage in the proventriculus distends the stomach walls and weakens the stomach muscles.

Signs: Ducklings three to eight weeks of age are the most likely to become infested. They become listless and lose interest in eating. At the same time, they often make retching motions while shaking their heads violently. After a few days, they succumb to weakness.

Treatment: When worms have been positively identified as the cause of death of one or more young ducklings, the rest of the flock can be saved through immediate veterinary treatment with deworming medications. Ducklings that survive an infestation harbor only a few of the parasites but keep eliminating worm eggs in their droppings.

Prevention: The most effective hygienic measure to prevent worm infestation is to keep the ducklings off bodies of water where the worms are established; instead, they should swim on artificial ponds without water fleas. Once the ducks are fully grown, the worms no longer pose a danger.

Egg Binding

Cause: A number of possible causes exist as to why a duck may be unable to pass an egg. The egg may be abnormally large or misshapen, or it may have too soft a shell. The condition often occurs in overweight ducks, ducks laying their first eggs, or ducks that have been overly productive in the past. It can also be the result of environmental factors such as a rapid and dramatic change in temperature. Eggs that lack the hard shell covering the egg skin adapt elastically to the wavelike contractions of the oviduct muscles without moving downward. Big eggs get stuck because of their size.

Signs: A duck in this predicament often sits on the ground very straight in "penguin position," ruffles her feathers, and keeps her eyes shut. The lower abdomen protrudes balloonlike and feels hot. The caudal feathers may be dirty with a sticky discharge, feces, and sand.

Treatment: Take the duck to the veterinarian for immediate treatment.

What Can You Do to Help a Sick Duck?

If you keep your duck yard clean and feed your ducks a healthy diet, you should be able to prevent many illnesses because poor sanitary conditions are linked to many duck diseases. If illness breaks out in your flock, take these steps to protect your healthy birds:

1. Isolate sick ducks from the rest of the flock. This is done to prevent the sickness from spreading to the other ducks and to provide quiet for the sick one.

2. Plan ahead and make sure you have an "infirmary" ready. There, place the bird on a soft surface, like a rubber mat, and give it a shallow dish with food and one with water within bill's reach. If the duck refuses to eat, you may have to force-feed it.

Chapter Seven

Raising Ducks

Necessary Conditions

Some very basic differences exist between raising utility ducks and raising ornamental ducks. The former is a commercial enterprise, while the latter activity is confined almost exclusively to duck fanciers.

Utility Ducks

Most utility ducks are raised to be sold as roast ducklings, while some are used as breeding stock to maintain and improve individual breeds. Egg and down production for human use is insignificant compared to the meat industry.

For duck raising to be economically productive, you must follow certain rules:

• Use only fully grown stock for breeding. Heavyweight breeds such as Rouen and Aylesbury ducks reach sexual maturity at one year of age; Pekin ducks and other medium-heavy to light breeds are fully mature at six months.

• Establish your breeding groups. A breeding group consists of a drake and several females. One drake and two ducks are called a trio; a drake with four or five ducks are a pen. The highest fertility rates are achieved in light breeds with four or five ducks per drake and in heavy breeds with two or three ducks per drake. Combine the birds in the fall so they can get used to each other before breeding season.

• Since heavy breeds achieve better fertility rates if they mate in the water, provide at least a small swim basin in their enclosure.

• Breeder birds should conform to their breed standard; that is, they should have all the qualities that the standard for that particular breed calls for. This includes not only coloration of the plumage but also meat quality, egg production, and weight.

As a general rule, you can assume that breeding ducks of both sexes are still productive in their fifth year. Females start laying at about 140 to 180 days of age. Good breeder ducks should be lively birds that continually and actively search for food.

Here's a quick test you can perform: If a female's plumage is still smooth and hugs the body closely at the end of the laying period, this indicates she is a good layer. On the other hand, if the feathers remain wet a long time after bathing, this is a sign of a poor constitution, and many breeders assume the quality of the parents' constitution is reflected in the ducklings. This does not necessarily mean, however, that the ducklings of good parent birds are always strong and hardy, especially if the parent birds have not been adequately fed and were kept in runs that were too small for them. If the breeder birds are not cared for properly, the proportion of fertile eggs declines, embryos die within the eggs, and the ducklings that do hatch are weak. Remember all these factors before you blame poor hatching rates on faulty incubators.

Ornamental Ducks

In contrast to domestic ducks, ornamental ducks are essentially wild ducks and are monogamous. This is why ornamental ducks are always combined in pairs. Since each pair establishes its own territory during the courtship and laying period and defends this territory against other pairs, fights may break out in small enclosures. Although most of these conflicts do not end in fatalities, they are upsetting to the birds and can interfere with breeding so that no offspring are produced. On a larger body of water where potential antagonists have a chance to avoid each other, such problems are less frequent. But breeding success is most likely if only one pair of ducks is kept in an aviary.

Nest Sites

Wild Ducks

In their natural habitat, wild ducks lay their eggs hidden in bushes, large tufts of grass, stands of reeds, or other vegetation. Wood ducks and mandarin ducks always nest above ground in tree holes. Only the uniquely adaptable mallard will make its nest just about anywhere.

If you keep ornamental or wild ducks in aviaries or on ponds, make sure they have artificial nest sites (see Keeping Ducks in an Aviary, Keeping Ducks on a Pond, pages 45 and 46). If there are enough plants to provide cover, you can dig shallow hollows in the earth between them and cover the hollows with hay, straw, or dry leaves. Ducks often accept small doghouses, horizontally placed barrels, fruit crates, or a small A-frame made of a few boards—all kinds of shelters into which the birds can retreat—and use them for nesting.

Hole nesters, such as the wood duck and the mandarin duck, insist on nest boxes or cavities that are at least 20 inches (50 cm) off the ground even in captivity. Mount the boxes on posts, and provide access for birds whose wings are clipped by leaning a small wooden ladder or a split log against the box just below the entry hole.

Domestic Ducks

Of the many domestic duck breeds, only a few still brood their own eggs. Among these breeds are the call duck and the East Indie duck.

Ornamental ducks, such as these mandarin ducks, are monogamous and should be kept in pairs for breeding success.

Completely unrelated to these is the muscovy duck, which also broods its own eggs. Set up nests in the duck house for these broody ducks.

Since muscovies are hole nesters, their nests should be off the ground and reachable by way of a chicken ladder. Both the East Indie and the call duck nest on the ground. The best location for the nests is along the side and back walls of the building, where the ducks brood happily in flat crates that are filled with straw or hay.

The females of highly developed domestic breeds, on the other hand, have lost their brooding instinct almost entirely and simply drop their eggs wherever they happen to be. Some of them occasionally do lay eggs in a nest, but they are unreliable brooders or abandon the eggs altogether. You have to collect the eggs you find lying on the ground every day.

Extended Daylight = Extended Egg Production

Proper lighting can help bring breeding ducks into egg-laying condition. Increasing levels of daylight from January to June signal the ducks' bodies to begin the egg-laying process, while decreasing light levels from July to December indicate to the ducks that it's time to stop producing eggs. Supplement natural light with artificial light to expose ducks to 17 hours of total daylight in order to maintain optimal egg production.

Natural Incubation

Natural incubation means that the eggs are brooded by the duck that laid them or by a foster mother, such as another duck or a chicken.

Ornamental ducks are usually steady brooders unless they are disturbed by having to share their living space with too many other birds. It stands to reason that successful natural brooding and crowding of the duck enclosures are mutually exclusive. In unprotected areas, on the other hand, ducklings are exposed to many dangers because crows, magpies, martens, cats, and other predators all take their toll. That is why it is better not to let the natural mother brood her clutch and lead her young about in unprotected surroundings. Instead, put the eggs under a reliable foster mother, or brood the eggs artificially with the aid of an electric incubator (see Artificial Incubation, page 67).

Foster Mothers

Ducks as Foster Mothers

The muscovy duck is probably the most ideal duck foster mother. Muscovies get broody three times a year, are reliable brooders, and also mother the ducklings well. It is a good idea to have several muscovy ducks so that at least one of them is likely to be broody when the need arises. Call ducks have also proven to be good foster mothers, especially for clutches of small ornamental ducks.

Muscovies can also foster the eggs of utility ducks that have lost their brooding instinct. In large operations, artificial incubation is used for practical reasons.

A duck that serves as a foster mother has to lay her own eggs before she is ready to sit. In the case of muscovies, a clutch will consist of about 15 eggs. When the clutch is complete, replace it with the eggs of another species. The rule of thumb is that a foster mother duck should sit

Depending on the species, duck eggs will incubate anywhere between 21 and 35 days.

Here, the duckling bores a small hole in the egg with his egg tooth.

The duckling struggles his way out of the shell.

Exhausted from the hatching effort, baby ducklings usually just lie there for a little while.

The muscovy duck is especially good at fostering eggs from ornamental or utility ducks. Some of them become adoptive mothers to other poultry species, such as chickens.

on no more eggs than she can cover with her body, which is between 15 and 20 for the muscovy duck.

Chickens as Foster Mothers

It is common practice today to take duck eggs away from broody chickens shortly before hatching and place them in a hatching incubator. Depending on the size of the eggs and the breed or species of duck, a broody chicken can cover a clutch of 8 to 10 duck eggs. Moisten the eggs regularly with a plant mister because a chicken's plumage is drier than that of a duck. You can do the spraying when the chicken leaves the nest to eat and drink. Since a chicken is unable to grease the ducklings with oil from her

uropygial gland (see Dry Plumage, page 57), keep the ducklings away from swimming water for the first few days.

Some chickens that serve as duckling foster mothers kill the ducklings when they hatch because the voices of the baby ducks sound unfamiliar to them. Since it tends to be the same chickens that keep killing ducklings, eliminate these birds as foster mothers.

Occasionally, broody chickens leave the a clutch of duck eggs prematurely because chicken eggs take only 21 days to hatch, whereas duck eggs require 21 to 35 days of incubation, depending on the species. In this case, too, place the eggs in an incubator until the ducklings hatch.

Artificial Incubation

Duck eggs can be artificially brooded in electric incubators. There are two basic types: still-air and forced-air incubators. The first type is designed for one layer of eggs, while in the second, several trays of eggs are stacked on top of each other.

Sometimes people speak of starter incubators and hatching incubators. Both can be of either of the two types mentioned above; they differ from each other only in function. Eggs are placed in a starter incubator at the beginning of incubation and left there until shortly before they are due to hatch. Then they are placed in a hatching incubator, where the ducklings actually emerge from their shells. This method of using two incubators has proven advantageous for practical and hygienic reasons.

The Eggs

Collecting the Eggs

If you decide not to let your female ornamental ducks sit on their eggs, you will have to remove the eggs from the nests every day, but always leave a chicken egg or a fake egg in the nest. This way, the laying ornamental female will not become discouraged and will go on laying in the same nest. Because ducks keep laying longer when a full clutch fails to accumulate, you will end up with many more eggs than you would if you let the natural mother sit on the clutch.

Marking the Eggs

Any egg that is to be incubated should have the name of the breed or species and the laying date marked on the shell. This allows you to keep track of each egg and the productiveness of the ducks. It also makes it possible for you to make up clutches combining eggs of the same breed or species. In the case of ornamental ducks, this is important because the eggs of many wild species are so similar that it would be impossible to tell them apart without the date written on them. On commercial duck farms, where generally only one breed is raised, the laying date is all that has to be noted.

Washing the Eggs

Domestic duck eggs are often smeared with wet droppings, which have to be carefully washed off. The droppings may harbor pathogens that could develop and multiply in the humid, warm environment of the incubator and later lead to massive losses among the hatched ducklings (see Salmonellosis, page 57).

Place dirty eggs in a 0.1 percent potassium permanganate solution, which softens the caked dirt and kills many of the germs in it, for a few minutes. Afterward, wipe off the eggs carefully with a soft sponge. If you run a large duck-raising operation, you may want to routinely fumigate all eggs with formalin before placing them in the incubator.

Storing the Eggs

Eggs collected from ornamental and commercial ducks are stored in

Proper Incubation Temperatures for Duck Eggs

Day	Temperature	Relative Humidity	Incubator
1–24	99.7 to 100°F (37.6 to 37.8°C)	50 to 70 percent	Starter
25–28	99.1 to 99.5°F (37.3 to 37.5°C)	70 to 90 percent	Hatching

a special room before they are incubated. This is necessary, first of all, because you have to accumulate enough eggs to form a clutch before you can give them to a broody bird or place them in an incubator. More importantly, the tiny embryos inside the eggs start developing slowly even below the optimal brooding temperature of 100°F (37.8°C), and incorrect storage temperatures and air conditions can lead to premature death of embryos.

The room where the eggs are stored should be 59° to 65°F (15° to 18°C) and have a humidity level of 70 percent. During the warm part of the year, the shorter the waiting period before incubation, the greater the proportion of eggs that hatch. Duck eggs lose their viability more quickly than chicken eggs do and ideally should not be stored longer than a week before incubation. During the waiting period, turn the eggs at least three times per day. Before the eggs are given to a foster mother or put in an incubator, keep them in a warmer room for several hours because a sudden temperature change can prove fatal to the embryo.

Candling Eggs

Candling is done to see if eggs are fertile and later to find out in good time if an embryo has died and the egg is beginning to rot. Duck eggs should be candled on the 7th, 14th, and 22nd days of incubation. Candle eggs in a darkened room with a commercially available egg candler.

• Infertile eggs show up clear with the yolk appearing only faintly. The air space cell has increased in size.

• Fertile eggs show a small, dark spot with tiny blood vessels branching out from it. From the 14th day on, they are opaque and appear almost black.

• An embryo that has started to develop and then dies appears as a dark, floating blot that is sometimes stuck to the inside of the shell.

Incubation Factors

The six most important factors affecting incubation are temperature, air, humidity, rotation, turning, and cooling.

Temperature probably has the most critical effect on chick development. In an artificial incubator, temperature can be precisely regulated by means of a thermostat. The table on page 68 shows the exact incubation temperatures necessary for duck eggs.

Air flow carries heat, humidity, and fresh air to the different parts of the incubator. To achieve as even an air circulation as possible, forced-air incubators are equipped with vents and fans. There are incubators with rapid and with slower air circulation. For incubating duck eggs, slower air circulation seems to work better. Set the fan in such a way that the air is renewed eight to ten times per hour. Duck embryos have a higher metabolism rate than chicken embryos. The temperature and the relative air humidity should be set as shown on page 68 for eggs of domestic ducks and mallards.

Humidity inside the incubator is regulated by a contact thermometer that is connected to a humidifier. If your incubator is not equipped with this kind of automatic system, moisten the eggs once a day with a plant mister filled with lukewarm water. Increased humidity toward the end of incubation is very important if waterfowl eggs are artificially incubated. That is why the relative air humidity is set higher in the hatching incubator than in the starting incubator.

Rotation refers to the way a mother duck keeps moving the eggs around with her bill. Thus, the eggs that were on the outside of the clutch are gradually moved to the center and vice versa, with the result that the brooding warmth is shared equally. In an attempt to imitate this system, the breeder should move the eggs around in the incubator every day and turn them at the same time.

Turning the eggs is crucial for the normal development of the embryos. A mother duck turns her eggs every couple of hours, which, during an incubation period of 26 days, adds up to some 500 turnings. She turns them 90 degrees, 180 degrees, and 360 degrees. If the eggs were not turned, the embryos would get stuck to the yolks and to the egg membranes and would perish.

Eggs that are artificially incubated need to be turned several times a day, too. Some incubators have timers and electric motors that automatically tilt the egg trays every hour or two, first 90 degrees to one side, then 90 degrees to the other. If your incubator lacks these technical refinements, turn the eggs manually a minimum of three times a day and always by 180 degrees. To keep track of which eggs have been turned and which have not, it is helpful to mark each egg with different symbols on opposite sides, for instance, 1 and 2 or M and E. By starting out with the same symbol on the top of every egg, you can see at a glance if you have neglected to turn one. Four days before the hatching date, the eggs should no longer be turned, and they should be moved from the starter to the hatching incubator.

Cooling the incubating eggs is also important. In nature, the brooding duck leaves her clutch once a day for a half hour to eat and eliminate,

Incubation Periods for Different Kinds of Ducks

Since the incubation period for ducks varies from 21 to 35 days, it is important to know how long your duck eggs will take to hatch. The following table gives the different time periods:

Species	Period
Mallard and domestic ducks descended from them	26 to 29 days
Spotbill duck	26 to 28 days
Pintail	21 to 23 days
Gadwall	25 to 27 days
Falcated teal	25 to 26 days
Northern shoveler	25 to 27 days
European wigeon	22 to 25 days
American wigeon	22 to 25 days
Chiloë wigeon	24 to 25 days
Green-winged teal	21 to 23 days
Garganey	21 to 25 days
Cinnamon teal	24 to 25 days
Blue-winged teal	24 to 26 days
Baikal teal	23 to 26 days
Bahama pintail	25 to 26 days
Silver teal	24 to 26 days
Ringed teal	23 days
Mandarin duck	31 days
Wood duck	28 to 32 days
Muscovy duck	35 days
Red-crested pochard	26 to 28 days
Rosy-bill	27 to 29 days
European pochard	24 to 26 days
Tufted duck	23 to 25 days
Ferruginous duck	25 to 27 days
Ruddy duck	23 to 26 days
Common goldeneye	27 to 32 days

and the eggs may cool down by 14 to 18°F (8 to 10°C). This brief daily drop in temperature not only has no harmful effect on the embryos but, on the contrary, improves their vigor because it allows for an increased exchange of gases through the porous eggshell. More oxygen enters through the pores of the egg membrane and into the vascular system of the embryo, and more carbonic acid is dissipated by the same route.

In artificial incubation, we attempt to duplicate this process. From the 10th day until the chicks start pipping, the eggs are periodically allowed to cool. This is done by opening the incubator two or three times a day for 15 to 20 minutes, leaving the fans running, to let the eggs cool down to 86°F (30°C). Always cool the eggs before moving and turning them. Experiments comparing eggs that are cooled and eggs that are not cooled during artificial incubation have clearly shown that the first method produces superior hatching results.

Proper position of the egg at hatching time is also crucial for normal hatching. Slightly raise (no more than 45 degrees) the blunt end with the air chamber. This is the easiest position for the duckling to break through the cell membrane so that it can breathe in the oxygen. If the pointed end were raised, the duckling would try to turn its head up but would be unable to do so and would suffocate for lack of air.

Hatching Ducklings

Depending on the species, a duckling breaks through the inner membrane that separates it from the air cell some time between the 21st and the 35th day of incubation. The duckling uses its egg tooth—a small, hard bump on the upper mandible—to puncture the membrane. Now the duckling has enough air to breathe; the air cell or air chamber at this

point takes up a fourth of the space inside the shell, having increased as moisture evaporated.

Vocal contact: Ducklings begin to breathe and chirp three days before they actually hatch. If they are naturally brooded, the mother duck responds to their chirps with soft sounds of her own and thus establishes vocal contact with her offspring very early. In an incubator, the ducklings have to make do without their mother's voice, but this lack has no negative effect on the hatching process or the ducklings' later development.

Breaking out of the shell: When the duckling is ready to emerge from the shell, it presses its bill with the egg tooth against the inside wall on the blunt end of the egg and bores a small hole through it. This is called *pipping*. Once the initial hole is made, the duckling continues pipping and at the same time slowly

Wild ducklings such as this mallard that have lost their mother can be difficult to rear because of their fear of humans.

rotates inside the shell by pushing with its left leg until a ring-shaped crack develops and the top of the shell is ready to lift off. Kicking with both feet, the duckling eventually makes its way out of the shell and then just lies there for a while, exhausted by the effort. The damp down that clings to its body dries off within 30 to 60 minutes in the incubator or under a mother duck's wings, and then the duckling appears the way we all picture ducklings, cute and fluffy. The hatching process from the beginning of pip-ping until the duckling leaves the egg takes about 12 hours.

Artificial Rearing

Wild Ducklings

Newly hatched wild ducklings hide timidly when the incubator door is first opened. If you try to pick one up, it may jump out in a flash and quickly scuttle across the floor to a dark corner, where it will hunker down motionless. This is an indication that the predator image, or the panic response at the approach of a large creature, is inborn. Later on, the ducklings will become accustomed to their caretaker and even take food from his or her hand; however, they don't like to be touched and don't follow that person around. Wild ducklings that have lost their mother when several days old are difficult to rear because of their great fear of humans. They keep trying to escape, are extremely shy, and accept food only reluctantly. The chances of helping them survive, therefore, are slim.

The Brooder Box

Whether you are dealing with wild or domestic ducklings, you will have to move them from the incubator into a brooder box as soon as they are dry. The brooder box should be built of plywood, masonite, or rugged cardboard, and it should measure 36 inches long, 20 inches wide, and 24 inches high (90 × 50 × 60 cm). The box should be warmed with a heat lamp.

If wild ducklings are being raised, the top of the brooder box must be covered with chicken wire because even tiny ducklings can jump very high and are amazingly good at climbing up the corners of a box. Ducklings of hole-nesting species, such as wood or mandarin ducks, have tiny, sharp claws that enable them to climb up the walls of the tree holes where they were hatched so that they can jump to the ground. The walls of a wooden box or vertical wire mesh, therefore, are not much of an obstacle for them.

Need for Warmth

During the first few weeks of life, ducklings need a lot of warmth. Only the young of a few species of diving ducks are an exception because they are covered with thick, woolly down. All other ducklings should be raised in a room that is 86°F (30°C). The temperature inside the brooder box should be 90 to 95°F (32 to 35°C). Measure the warmth the heat lamp emits at the distance where the ducklings are, and make sure that the ducklings have a chance to get away from the lamp's rays. The bottom of the brooder box has to be warm, too. This is accomplished by placing an electric heating unit, like the ones used to keep food warm, underneath the brooder box.

As the ducklings grow older, they need less heat. By the second week, 77°F (25°C) is warm enough, and after that, the temperature can be lowered even faster than for baby chickens. By the time they are four weeks old, ducklings no longer need any artificial heat, even at night, as long as the weather is warm.

No Single Ducklings

Never try to raise a single duckling because ducklings tend to miss their siblings more than their mother. Try to have a flock of birds that is approximately the same age and size. If some are younger and smaller, they are often pushed away from the feeder by bigger ones and thus remain weak and stunted.

Need for Water

Ducklings need a permanent supply of fresh, clean drinking water to maintain good health. They also need to be able to completely dunk their heads into the water for cleaning and maintenance, but they should not be able to swim in it because it will quickly become contaminated with droppings. Watch ducklings carefully to make sure they are consuming enough water because ducklings can be prone to dehydration. Signs of a dehydrated duckling include a bird that staggers or goes into convulsions. Consult your veterinarian about what steps to take to revive a dehydrated duckling *before* the problem arises so you will know what to do.

Sanitation

Line the brooder box with a thick layer of absorbent paper or sheets for the first days. Keep changing the paper or cloths frequently because ducklings digest food quickly. Meticulous cleanliness is important. Also remove any leftover or spilled food because fungi can develop on it, and if the ducklings inhale fungal spores, they may become ill and die (see Aspergillosis, page 59).

Swimming Opportunity

Since the plumage of ducklings hatched in an incubator isn't water repellent, offer drinking water to these ducklings in shallow dishes for the first two or three days. In the sec-ond week, give them a swimming basin with ½ inch (1 cm) of water in it. At about two weeks of age, the plumage begins to become water resistant, and the ducklings produce enough oil in their uropygial glands to take care of the entire plumage (see Dry Plumage, page 57).

Ducklings that are raised for market should not be allowed to swim but should receive only enough water for bathing.

Natural Rearing

If you let a mother duck of an ornamental species brood and raise her own ducklings, you will witness some wonderful scenes from animal life. Unfortunately, however, a large number of predators are interested in a tasty meal of duckling, so the ducklings are gone in a few days. The only alternative is to have the ducks breed and raise their young in an aviary (see Keeping Ducks in an Aviary, page 45).

Using a muscovy or a call duck as a foster mother for ornamental ducklings is comparable in every respect to letting their natural mother brood them.

Chickens rarely chaperone ducklings once they have hatched, but broody chickens still come in handy for incubating duck eggs until they are almost ready to hatch, at which time they are moved to an incubator.

Chapter Eight
Understanding Ducks

The Adaptable Bird

Ducks are among some of the world's most adaptable birds. They have learned to live in the Arctic tundra as well as along the rivers of tropical rain forests, on inland streams with whitewater rapids, as well as on the cold, stormy islands along the Antarctic. Few other bird families on our planet have succeeded in finding niches for themselves in such a variety of habitats. In order to survive, the ducks had to adapt to the different environmental conditions they found, and in the process, a number of genera, species, and subspecies evolved.

Scientifically speaking, the duck family is a subfamily (Anatinae) of the family Anatidae, which includes swans and geese as well as ducks. The duck family is further broken down into eight tribes: *Tadornini*, which are the five genera and 14 species of shelducks and allies; *Tachyerini*, which is the one genera and four species of steamer ducks; *Cairini*, which are the nine genera and 13 species of perching ducks and allies; *Merganettini*, which is the torrent duck (*Merganetta armata*); *Anatini*, which are the four genera and 40 species of dabbling ducks; *Aythyini*, which are the two genera and 15 species of pochards; *Mergini*, which are the seven genera and 18 species of mergansers and allies; and *Oxyurini*, which are three genera and eight species of stifftails.

Since most ducks are gregarious and coexist peacefully outside of the breeding season, you can keep birds of different species together on the same body of water. Toward the end of the 19th century, naturalists noticed and began to take advantage of this unusual opportunity to observe a number of related bird species interact in a limited area. Their observations and reports provided important groundwork for the modern study of ethology, the study of animal behavior. The study of duck behavior has yielded results that are both fascinating and surprising, and they form the subject matter of this chapter, which is intended to help readers gain a better understanding of these interesting birds.

Where Do Geese and Swans Fit In?

Geese and swans are members of the same scientific family as ducks—Anatidae. Swans are members of the subfamily Cygninae, and geese are members of the subfamily Anserinae—so they are somewhat like cousins in a human family.

The family Anatidae contains all swimming birds that have webbed feet and lamellate bills, or bills with toothlike edges on them. These birds have short legs, four-toed feet, short tails, longish necks, and moderately long wings. Most of them nest on the ground, and they molt their flight feathers simultaneously, which leaves them unable to fly for a certain part of the summer each year.

Larger than ducks but smaller than swans, geese are the intermediate members of the Anatidae family. Male and female geese look almost identical, as opposed to duck species in which males and females sport different plumage. Their bills are slightly more pointed than ducks, and they feed more on land than either ducks or swans do. They especially enjoy grazing in meadows and fields. Geese are frequently found on farms, where they can be raised for feathers, eggs, or meat. Some farmers keep geese as feathered watchdogs because the birds will sound an alarm if they see a stranger coming onto their property. They are hardy, adaptable birds that require modest accommodations in order to thrive.

When selecting geese, keep in mind that ganders (the male birds) can be more aggressive than geese (the females). Geese need other geese for companionship, so don't keep a lone bird on your property. Geese are among the most faithful of mates—they form lifetime pair bonds that can last 25 years or more and successfully raise their young.

Swans are further distinguished by their large size and stately appearance. Their extremely long, graceful necks also set them apart from other members of the Anatidae family. Like geese, males and females resemble one another when mature. They are usually white in color when mature (except, of course, for the black swans), and they feed on aquatic plants, insects, and mollusks by tipping and dabbling in shallow fresh water. Swans are not usually found on farms, but they can be seen at parks and zoos across North America, and some breeders will sell them directly to individuals with large ponds that can accommodate a swan's needs.

Handling a Goose or Swan

To handle a goose or swan, catch it by the neck, rather than the leg. Hold the bird's neck and draw the bird's body close to your own, wrapping your free arm around the bird's wings as you pull it toward you. Pick up the bird and move it to the side of your body so its head and neck stick out from under your arm.

Bird Words

	Ducks	Geese	Swans
Adult Male	drake	gander	cob
Adult Female	duck	goose	pen
Offspring	duckling	gosling	cygnet
Group	Bunch, brood, knob, raft, skein, string, mob, paddling, plump, sord, sore, team, waddling	gaggle, clutch, flock, line, skein, nide, wedge	flock, bevy, bank, eyrar, drift, game, herd, sownder, team, wedge, whiteness

How Ducks Get Their Food

Dabbling Ducks

Ducks like the familiar mallard are called dabbling ducks. This means that they find their food in the water as well as on land. As they swim, dabbling ducks grab floating food items from the water's surface, pick off plant particles, and sift through the mud at the bottom of shallow waters, straining out tiny food organisms with their bills. When they feed at the bottom, they "upend"—that is, they tip their bodies forward so that the front half is submerged while the back half sticks up in the air. They stay balanced in this position by treading water. Just about everybody has probably seen ducks "stand on their heads" in this way.

Dabbling ducks can feed on the bottom of waters up to 19 inches (48 cm) deep and can stay underwater an average of 4.2 seconds at a time. They submerge completely only when they sense danger or when taking a vigorous bath.

Diving Ducks

Certain duck varieties get almost all their food by diving. Tufted ducks sometimes dive down as far as 40 feet (12 m). Diving ducks look for food, such as mussels, clams, snails, and worms in the lake or stream bed.

Deep diving is not easy for a duck because it is very light-bodied, which means a strong force always pushes the duck toward the water surface. How does a duck overcome it? To increase its specific gravity, a duck exhales before diving and presses its feathers close to its body. Before actually diving, the duck tosses its head back and pulls its feet upward and forward, which makes the duck's back end dip

Larger than a duck (right) but smaller than a swan, a goose (left) is an intermediate member of the Anatidae family.

Dabbling ducks such as the mallard look for their food on both land and water. Here, a male mallard forages at the edge of a pond.

deeper into the water. Now comes the actual "dive." The duck thrusts its head forward into the water, and pushes back hard with its feet at the same time. Once underwater, the duck presses its wings close to its body. The wings are used only for increasing speed when fleeing from danger.

When a duck dives in search of food, it propels itself downward with even motions of its webbed feet. The higher up the feet, the steeper the dive. When the feet are held lower, the body glides in an almost horizontal position and at a slight downward tilt. As soon as the paddling motions of the feet stop and the head is raised, the duck shoots to the water surface like a cork. The records for staying underwater longest are held by tufted ducks with 41 seconds for the drake and 36.8 seconds for the female.

Feeding on Land

Ducks forage not only in the water but also on land. The mallard is one kind of duck that likes to feed on young grass and tender leaves as it grazes. It is adept at stripping grass seeds from their panicles and swallows acorns, beechnuts, and berries whole. It also eats insects, snails, and other small creatures—in short, anything it runs across that its bill can handle.

Sometimes you may see young ducks leap up and race across the water this way and that. They are chasing tiny insects, which make up their main fare during the first couple of weeks. When big hatches of mayflies or mosquitoes occur, grown ducks can be seen performing these acrobatic feats, too.

A Duck's Bill, the Perfect Sieve

Ducks sift the mud at the bottom of shallow waters through their bills and eat the tiny organisms that live there. They couldn't do this if their bills weren't highly specialized for this task. The broad, flattened upper mandible is covered with soft skin that has many sensitive taste buds distributed over it, especially near the tip. The nerves leading to the taste buds run through tiny pores or canals in the bone of the mandible. Because of this, the tactile sense is extremely sensitive in the bill and makes it easy for ducks to sense and catch tiny organisms in cloudy water and mud.

Straining: Along the outer edge of the lower mandible, as well as on the inner edge of the protruding upper mandible, are many fine parallel horny plates, called *lamellae*, arranged in a comblike pattern. The tongue is fringed with similar lamellae along the sides. When a duck picks up a mouthful of mud, it closes its bill and pushes the water out with its tongue, forcing it out between the lamellae. The lamellae retain the solid matter as the water is strained out. The duck's sensitive tongue quickly distinguishes what is edible, and the inedible mud particles are discarded.

A duck has a skin-covered nail on the end of its bill that helps it hold onto large or slippery pieces of food.

When a duck sifts through organic matter floating on the water's surface, its tongue serves as a sucking mechanism. It draws a stream of water in at the tip of the bill and lets it flow out through the lamellae at the back of the bill, where usable food particles are caught.

The nail: At the tip of the of the upper mandible is a small hook called the nail. It is the only part of

Ducks have fine horny plates called lamellae along the edges of their bills. The lamellae enable the ducks to strain mud from the bottom of ponds and lakes in order to eat the tiny organisms that live in the mud.

the bill with a tough hard skin, and the duck uses it to hold big or slippery pieces of food securely.

How Ducks Bathe

The bathing ritual, as we may rightly call it, almost always consists of a definite sequence of motions. First, the duck dips its head into the water and splashes water over its back with sideward head motions. While the water flows down the back, the duck spreads its tail and lifts one or both wings with repeated fanning of the primaries. This phase of the ritual may last for 10 minutes or more. Then the duck lowers its breast deep into the water, often while pulling its head in close to its body. At the same time, the body tilts more or less to the side and every so often rolls over in a sideways somersault.

When the duck has regained its normal swimming position, it starts

Between full baths, ducks keep themselves clean by preening their feathers and occasionally scratching.

"beating its wings." This means that the duck beats down hard on the water, first with one wing and then with the other.

This phase of the ritual is followed by the most eye-catching activity, namely a period of wild dashing across the water and diving. Once one duck starts doing this, others often follow. After diving several times with open wings, the ducks scoot across the water, wings flapping wildly, take to the air briefly, and then plunge back into the water. They move around on the water this way for some time, splashing, diving, and flying with such vigor that a casual observer might easily interpret the action as aggressive chases. In fact, the ducks are simply indulging in one of their favorite pastimes, namely, bathing.

Ducks take full baths like this, which can last 10 to 20 minutes, once or twice a day when the weather is sunny. On overcast days, they don't usually bathe at all. Between baths, ducks keep themselves clean by pulling their wing, flank, and tail feathers through their bills quickly and forcefully. The birds often scratch themselves, too.

Preening

When you watch a duck preening itself meticulously and almost endlessly, you might think all its fussy plumage care a bit excessive. But keeping the feathers in top condition is crucial to survival because the plumage has to keep out cold and wetness. To function effectively, the duck has to arrange and oil its feathers at regular, short intervals, and this task is usually taken care of right after bathing.

When a duck leaves the water, its first concern is to dry its plumage. Shaking the body makes drops of water fly off in all directions and causes the feathers to settle in their proper places. The process starts with the tail, which the duck shakes vigorously while raising the small contour feathers, then the shaking moves forward over the slightly raised body all the way to the neck. At the same time, the duck vibrates its wings in place and rotates its raised head several times with the bill making a circle.

Ducks also scratch themselves with their bills and toes. This activity probably helps get moisture out of the deeper layers of the plumage. All these preening motions help the barbules interlock with microscopically small hooks so that the feathers stay in place and are properly fluffed up. This way, enough air is trapped in the plumage so that it continues to serve as a warm insulating coat covering the entire body.

The Function of the Oil Gland

When the feathers are dry enough, the duck begins to oil them. First, it rubs its chin, cheek, and crown over the bared oil gland just above the tail,

Preening is a normal and important part of a duck's daily care routine. Preening helps maintain the bird's feathers so they keep out water and cold drafts.

then it draws the wing and tail feathers quickly through its bill. In this process, the duck greases its bill and the entire hind part of its body. Working this way, a duck can pick up oil from the gland up to seven times in five minutes, reaching back alternately on the right and left side.

The females of some duck species stop oiling their plumage when they settle down on their eggs and don't start again until just before the ducklings are due to hatch. This freshly distributed oil is automatically transferred from the mother's feathers to the down of the newly hatched ducklings. Ducklings do have functional oil glands at the time of hatching, and the behavior of oiling the feathers is inborn, but apparently the glands aren't productive enough at first, so that the mother has to help out (see Dry Plumage, page 57).

Rest and Sleep

All vertebrates need periods of rest and sleep of various length. Ducks are diurnal as well as nocturnal, alternating periods of activity lasting roughly 45 to 75 minutes with rest periods of about 30 to 45 minutes. Ducks are most quiescent in the middle of the day and most active at night and in the early morning hours. Ducks that live in captivity have learned to change their routine because they are fed during the day and have to eat the food quickly before free-flying birds, such as crows, gulls, pigeons, or sparrows, get to it.

Speaking Duck

According to experts, only female ducks "quack." Drakes have a quieter, more throaty call. The only exception to this rule is the muscovy duck, which squeaks or whistles to communicate.

Ducks alternate rest periods with periods of activity during the day. Ducks tend to rest in the middle of the day and be active in the morning and late afternoon.

Unconfined wild ducks behave like all wild birds and adhere to a definite routine if they live in a natural environment and without human interference. They rest or sleep from about 9 to 11 in the morning, bathe and preen themselves around noon, and spend most of the afternoon resting. At dusk, they become more active, and most of the night and into the forenoon of the next day they are busy searching for food.

Wild ducks spend their resting periods and their feeding periods in different waters. They usually fly from their resting quarters to their feeding waters after sunset and return in the morning. The nightly foraging is interrupted by short rest periods. When it is too dark to see, they rely on their ability to taste and touch with their tongues and the skin of their bills. Since most inland water frequented by ducks is opaque, sight is of no great use in dabbling or diving for food.

Mallards and other dabbling ducks often spend the night on inland fields and meadows far from bodies of water. Here, they are safe from raptors and hunters, and all they have to watch out for are foxes and martens. In the open country, they can escape these enemies by flying straight up into the air.

Rest Positions

Ducks on land rest either by sitting on the ground or by standing on one leg. But they always keep a sharp eye on their surroundings. Since several of them often rest together, at least one bird can always be on guard. On the water, resting ducks let themselves drift with their bills tucked deep into the innermost feathers of the second wing segment. One leg is usually resting, pulled up next to the body, while the other paddles every so often to keep the body moving in the same direction.

We know very little about actual sleep in ducks, but we can assume with some degree of certainty that short periods of light sleep alternate with periods of wakefulness, and we are probably safe in asserting that wild ducks cannot afford a deep sleep.

On the water, a resting duck drifts with its bill tucked deeply into its wing feathers. The duck alternates resting its legs by paddling with one while resting the other.

Escape from Enemies

Ducks resting or foraging on land head for the water as quickly as they can if they sense danger. Since they are able to rise straight up into the air, they do not have much trouble getting away from predators such as foxes, dogs, cats, and martens. When they are pursued on the water, dabbling ducks such as our familiar mallard can dive out of sight just as fast as true diving ducks. When they dive to get away from some danger, ducks use their wings underwater for speed. They can change directions abruptly underwater, then surface again in places where their enemies are not looking for them.

In heavily settled areas, few animal predators are left that can attack ducks. Sea eagles have become so rare in central Europe, for instance, that they no longer represent a threat. If a sea eagle does hunt a duck, it follows the diving and surfacing bird until the duck finally tires and can be captured easily.

Diversionary behavior: Like many mother birds, female ducks try to divert a predator's attention away from their young. A duck mother feigns lameness and injury, hoping to distract an enemy. Fluttering and reeling, she lures the predator away from the nest by drawing attention to herself, then she suddenly makes her escape by taking off into the air.

Social Behavior

Ducks are extremely social birds when they are not engaged in

Healthy, well-maintained feathers help protect ducks against cold weather.

breeding and rearing young. It is this sociable quality that makes them so suitable for captivity. The various species that winter in North America often gather together in huge aggregations consisting of thousands of pairs and some unattached birds that try to join the crowd. These aggregations dissolve again with the arrival of spring, when pairs take off for the breeding grounds.

One important part of social behavior is the ability to communicate with others, which ducks do quite easily. British researchers reported in mid-2004 about the idea that ducks speak in dialects, much as humans do. Researcher Victoria de Rijke of Middlesex University compared ducks in central London to those found in rural Cornwall in order to answer the question: "Do ducks quack in the same way all over the world?"

"There are definite differences between them, with the London ducks noisier, laughing raucously, and the Cornish ones soft and chilled out," she told CNN. De Rijke said that the London ducks may need to be noisier in order to be heard over the background noise of a big city.

How Ducks Survive the Winter

If you see ducks swimming on open water surrounded by ice and snow or resting on lumps of ice, you may wonder how these birds manage to survive the cold. Cold winters are, of course, hard on the birds, and weak ones fail to survive.

Healthy ducks get ready for winter in the fall by putting on a subcutaneous layer of fat to keep them warm. Well-maintained, healthy feathers make an additional insulating coat that protects the ducks against hypothermia. When a duck closes its wings, the wings are often tucked into a kind of pocket formed by the feathers on the side of the breast, where they are protected from the water. But what about the feet and the delicate skin that forms the webs between the toes? These webs are not at all insensitive to the cold. That is why ducks usually paddle with one foot at a time when swimming in very cold water. The resting foot is tucked into a feather pocket, as into a fur muff, and it emerges only when the first foot has gotten too cold and needs warming up. Duck species from tropical regions often freeze their feet and webs if an inexperienced caretaker lets them swim in icy water. When ducks rest on a cold surface, such as an ice floe, they usually lower themselves onto their bellies. This way, their feet can warm up in the thick abdominal plumage.

It is also much more difficult to find sufficient food in the winter than during the warmer seasons. Healthy ducks such as the mallard can survive up to two weeks without eating, and in most situations this is probably enough time for the birds to locate waters with better food supply.

The Molt, a Time of Vulnerability

Birds replace their feathers during the molt. In ducks, molting is a rather complicated process that takes place in separate stages. The down the ducklings are hatched with begins to be replaced by small contour feathers at three weeks of age. At the same time, the big flight feathers begin to grow in. At four weeks of age, the breast is covered with feathers, and a few weeks later, the flight feathers are in place. Mallards reach this stage at seven and one half weeks of age, while Pekin ducks reach it in eight to ten weeks. By then, however, Pekin ducks are already much too heavy to fly and are therefore earthbound. If they are raised as market ducklings, they are slaughtered shortly before completing their juvenile molt because incoming feathers are very difficult to pluck (see page 127).

Drakes' Molt

Drakes, both wild and domestic, undergo an additional molt in the summer. In this molt, they lose their special nuptial plumage that they wear during courtship in the spring and put on a duller coat of feathers that renders them rather similar in appearance to females. This duller plumage is called eclipse plumage, and it is a camouflage plumage that provides additional protection for the drakes as they shed their flight feathers simultaneously and are flightless for three to four weeks. In the late summer, they undergo a new molt, which restores their nuptial plumage.

With the onset of the molt, the drakes leave their mates and the breeding grounds. They take off in the early summer, before the flight feathers begin to molt, and sometimes cover long distances to reach large bodies of open water where they join many other drakes to molt together. In migratory species, the drakes band together to fly to their winter territories.

Drakes (male ducks) such as this Northern pintail leave their mates in early summer before their flight feathers begin to molt. When they reach their winter territories, the drakes gather in large groups and molt their flight feathers together.

During the molt, diving ducks such as the common goldeneye feel safest on wide, open waters so they can see approaching predators and dive out of sight.

Wild female ducks cannot afford to molt their flight feathers so early because they are still brooding and rearing their young when the drakes take off to molt. Females don't shed their flight feathers until the ducklings can fly.

Being unable to fly for weeks is, of course, a highly dangerous situation for birds. That is why dabbling ducks become extremely shy during this period and hide in dense vegetation growing along the edges of water. Diving ducks, on the other hand, which rely on diving out of sight even

During courtship displays, a drake will display the curly "sex feathers" in the middle of his tail.

when they can fly, feel safest on wide, open waters during the molting period.

The Reproductive Period

Courtship Behavior

The courtship rituals of ducks are exceptionally fascinating. We will discuss them here, using the mallard duck as an example.

The grunt-whistle: Mated drakes start their courtship displays in the fall. Often, a group of them will congregate on the water for a communal display that the females gather to watch. The display starts with the drake raising his head feathers and pulling in his neck while repeatedly shaking his tail. Then the drake lifts his head and tosses it from side to side with increasing vigor, occasionally dipping his bill in the water. Suddenly, the drake jerks his body forward, lowers his head, and throws up drops of water with his bill, which sweeps rapidly back and forth across the water. Before the drake settles into a normal position, he emits a high whistle. This display is called the "grunt-whistle" and is always accompanied by tail shaking.

Sex feathers: In another phase of the display, all the drakes in a courtship group often simultaneously emit a long whistled note while lifting their heads high and then lowering them. At the same time, they raise their fanned tails high, which makes the drakes' bodies look strangely short and squat. The tips of the wings point straight up and the secondaries press upward. Seen from the side and in this posture, the drakes prominently display the tips of their wings and the curly feathers in the middle of their tails, which are the so-called "sex feathers." The drakes maintain this curious stance for only a few seconds; then they drop back to their normal posture but still keep their heads and necks raised.

Nod-swimming: Unattached drakes point their bills at any female that happens to be close, while bonded males address their displays exclusively to their chosen mates. A bonded male will swim around his mate in semicircles, extending his head forward low over the water while nodding vigorously. This display is called "nod-swimming."

Other phases: Then the drake raises his head again and turns the back of the neck with its bright green plumage toward the courted female. This is called the "turning-of-the-back-of-the-head." In the "down-up" phase, which follows next, the drake immerses his breast deep into the water before his head shoots up high and the bill raises a fountain of water drops. When his head is in its highest position, the courting drake whistles and then calls "raeb-raeb" with the bill tilted upward.

How Partners Get Acquainted with Each Other

Mallard females take a much more active part in wooing potential mates than the males do. An unattached drake joining a group of females is therefore in the enviable position of being able to choose and reject as he likes.

Inciting: Females ready to pick partners swim toward unattached drakes and display "inciting" behavior. When inciting, a female approaches a drake that appeals to her and at the same time makes threatening gestures across her shoulder toward any strange drake that happens to be swimming around in the vicinity. She will go through these motions even if the strange drake is not in the direction her gestures point toward. She accompanies the threatening gestures with a series of "gagg" notes that sound something like the bleating of goats. The duck does the threatening and calling with her head and back feathers flattened down smoothly.

"Inciting" is the most common and widespread form of love declaration among ducks. Female ducks use it first as a marriage proposal and later as a demonstrative affirmation of belonging to the drake. If, in

Female mallards take a more active role in courtship than do the drakes.

the courtship ritual, the unattached drake to whom the inciting was addressed responds by chasing the indicated strange drake away, this is a sign that he is accepting the female's overtures and is willing to "become engaged."

How an "Engaged" Pair Behaves

If the drake has taken a liking to the female—as his chasing away the strange drake indicates—he will stay close to her, drink to her, and pretend to preen himself. In pretend preening, or "preening-behind-the-wing," the drake raises his wings up at an angle to display the metallic green speculum on the wing and runs his bill over the edge of the secondaries, creating an audible rasping noise, then the two partners swim away from each other in opposite directions, and all contact between them seems to end. But whenever they meet again, they go through the motions described above, reaffirming their commitment to one another. Things can go on like this for days or weeks until the drake begins to follow the female around.

Now the two often have long tête-à-têtes during which she drinks to him and he returns the compliment, pretend-preens, and utters "raep-raep" calls. If a strange drake approaches her at this point, the female strongly incites her "suitor" to drive the intruder away as a demonstration of their commitment to each other. If he does her bidding, the bond between them can be regarded as established. Such bonds, as well

as firm pair formations, can take place any time from the end of August until winter.

Matrimony and Mating

"Married" ducks can be recognized in a winter flock by the fact that they spend more time near each other and stay closer together than the rest of the birds. They make threatening gestures toward other ducks, sometimes go off by themselves, and are generally inseparable. They rest huddled close together and behave as equals when feeding, and the male defends his mate if another drake happens to come too close. When the two partners get separated, the lost one keeps calling until they are reunited. When they leave the water in the spring, the female takes to the air first, while in the fall, the drake takes the initiative.

Mating takes place as early as the fall, even though the gamete-producing glands are not yet active. Presumably, these early matings serve to strengthen the pair bond. The actual mounting or "treading" is always preceded by mutual "head pumping." One partner suddenly moves the head down in several jerky movements, keeping the bill horizontal, then slowly raises it to its initial position. Then both partners start head pumping, which becomes more and more intense until the female is lying flat on the water. The drake now climbs onto her back, grabs the feathers on her nape with his bill, and pushes her into the water so deep that she is often almost entirely submerged. Then he presses his tail against the female's lifted tail from the side, and copulation takes place as the pair moves back and forth rhythmically.

Since the drake has a kind of a penis, the pair is able to stay locked together during copulation, which always takes place in the water. A few domestic ducks are also able to mate on the ground, but the fertilization rate under these conditions is often not as satisfactory.

As soon as the drake stops treading, he draws his head way back and emits a sharp whistle. Then he nod-swims around the female in a big circle, after which both start bathing and preening themselves while beating their wings.

Pursuit Chases in the Spring

In the spring, one often sees a single-flying female duck pursued by several drakes. What happens is that a strange drake tries to get hold of a female's tail by biting it, and the female's mate tries to do the same thing to the stranger. Such chases can go on for 3,000 feet (1,000 m) or so. They get started when mated drakes whose partners are brooding are trying to rape other females.

Even ducks that are brooding or leading their young are not safe from such pursuits by one or more drakes, but the chase is usually unsuccessful. When it is enacted on land, one

"Married" ducks stay closer to one another than they do to other birds. When separated, they call to one another until they are reunited.

gets a chance to observe the "gesture of repulsion" clearly. The female approaches the drakes with raised head and back feathers, holding her head way back on her shoulders, and she utters several sharp "gaek" calls with her bill wide open.

In animal parks, pinioned females that are unable to escape from flighted males sometimes drown when several drakes try to mount them.

Nest Building and Incubation

The drake and his mate select the nest site together, but the female does all the nest building. She pokes the ground with her bill on the selected spot, then lowers her breast into it and makes swimming motions with her feet to scrape leaves and loose earth toward the back. In this way, she gradually forms a shallow hole, which is smoothed out by the pressure of her breast as the duck slowly rotates in it. The duck uses only what is within reach of her bill in the nest; she will not carry nesting materials to the nest site.

When the female leaves the nest after she has started laying eggs, she heaps nesting material over the incomplete clutch and uses her bill to bury the eggs in the material. She waits until the clutch is complete before plucking down from her breast, which she distributes in a circle around the clutch. When she does this, she selects feathers that match the colors of the surroundings so that the clutch is well camouflaged.

When hatching time approaches and the female hears the first chirping of the ducklings inside their shells, she changes her incubating behavior. She turns the eggs much more frequently than before and emits soft calls herself. In this way, the ducklings are imprinted with the voice of their mother before they even hatch. When an enemy approaches, the mother gives warning calls, and the chirping stops. Shortly before the actual hatching, the mother begins oiling her plumage thoroughly so that the down of the newly hatched ducklings can absorb some of the secretion of the mother's oil gland and become water repellent right away. The mother eats most of the eggshells left behind by the ducklings, and the ducklings leave the nest for good six to twelve hours after hatching. Ducks are nidifugous birds, which means they are able to take care of themselves and leave the nest soon after hatching.

Mother and Her Ducklings

In dabbling ducks, the family attachment is quite close and lasts longer than in diving ducks. A mallard mother broods her ducklings for three to four weeks. Compared to chickens, ducklings need much less warmth from their mothers because their thick down coats protect them.

The mother neither feeds her ducklings nor does she teach them how to find food; she simply goes to places where she knows food is abundant. All the ducklings follow her single file, each copying what the one in front of it does.

Sibling cohesion: The fact that the ducklings stick primarily to each other and that the attachment to the mother is secondary makes them rather unique among baby birds. It doesn't matter if the mother is out of sight for most of them when she leads them. Even if the mother dies, this does not necessarily spell doom for the ducklings. The young of the tufted duck, for instance, fend for themselves when they are just a few days old and can, if the weather is not too bad, survive their mother's death within the first two weeks despite cold nights.

Mallard ducklings make their first flying attempts at seven and one half weeks of age. They are fully able to fly by the time they are eight weeks old. At this point, the bond between parent birds and their young dissolves completely.

Chapter Nine

Ornamental Ducks and Utility Ducks

In the following descriptions, the most popular ornamental ducks and utility ducks are introduced. The ornamental ducks fall into two groups—the dabbling ducks and the diving ducks—while utility or commercial ducks are usually divided into heavyweight, medium-weight, bantamweight, and lightweight breeds.

The following descriptions of species and breeds contain information on origin, appearance, habitat, requirements in captivity, breeding, egg laying, growth rate, and weight. The sizes given for wild or ornamental ducks indicate the length of an adult bird, measured from the tip of the bill to the tip of the tail.

Ornamental Ducks: Dabbling Ducks

Dabbling ducks, such as the mallard, can be recognized by how high they ride on the water and by the placement of the legs close to the middle of the body. Dabbling ducks feed in shallow water, frequently upending to seek food at the bottom.

Mallard Duck
Anas platyrhynchos

Size: 23 inches (58 cm)

Origin: Northern to central Eurasia; North America, especially in the Mississippi Valley. Has been introduced into the Caribbean and parts of Australia and New Zealand.

Description: The drake has an iridescent bottle-green head marked off by a white neck ring, a chocolate brown breast, a black rear end, including the tail coverts, and a dark blue speculum. The tail is white with four curled sex feathers in the middle. The bill is yellowish green; the legs, orange-red. The female is mostly brown and has an olive green bill.

On the waters of city parks, one often finds mallards whose blood is mixed with that of domesticated mallards. These birds tend to have differently colored plumage. The neck ring of the male is often absent, and white feathers are intermixed with the colors.

Habitat: Mallards live on all kinds of water, but they clearly prefer shallow lakes and ponds with an abundance of organic matter to feed on.

Male mallards are among the most easily recognized ducks, thanks to their bottle-green heads, brown breasts, and black rumps.

Some ducks are migratory, while others are resident in their lands of origin.

Captivity: The mallard has one of the most extensive breeding ranges in North America and is arguably the most beautiful of all the wild ducks. It is the stock from which all our domestic breeds (with the exception of the muscovy duck) are descended.

Many breeds of utility duck can trace their ancestry back to the mallard.

Mallards exist in large numbers and are extremely adaptable. They will settle on even the tiniest pond. If you have a small, ornamental garden pond with some water and marsh plants, you can almost count on a pair of mallards arriving in the spring on the lookout for a nesting site. Mallards living on ornamental duck ponds are often rather quarrelsome, and if their flight is not restrained, they tend to interbreed with related species, such as the spotbill duck. Raising purebred mallards is, therefore, possible only in an aviary. Since wild mallards seek out garden ponds on their own, there is generally little reason to clip their wings. Mallards are known to have lived as long as 22 to 29 years in captivity.

Breeding: Breeding mallards is easy. The birds accept just about any nesting site that is offered. The breeding season begins any time after mid-February, depending on the climate. A clutch consists of 7 to 11 eggs, which can be white, yellowish, grayish green, or light green. Incubation lasts 28 days. Rearing the ducklings is unproblematic; they start flying at seven and one-half weeks and reach sexual maturity before they are one year old.

Spotbill Duck

Anas poecilorhyncha

Size: 23½ inches (60 cm)

Origin: Indian peninsula, Sri Lanka, Burma, Korea, China, Mongolia, southeastern Siberia, and Japan.

Description: The two sexes differ only slightly in appearance. The

The northern pintail takes its name from its long, pointed tail feathers.

crown is dark brown, the head and neck are grayish white, and a band across the eyes is brown. The back and shoulder feathers are dark brown with gray borders. The speculum is green and has a white patch above it. The bill, which is black, has a yellow tip, and the base of the upper mandible is red.

Habitat: Shallow lakes and ponds with lush vegetation. Resident bird in their lands of origin.

Captivity: Spotbill ducks are attractive birds about the size of mallards that can winter over in North America with proper accommodation despite their tropical origins.

Breeding: Pure breeding is possible only in aviaries because spotbill ducks kept unrestrained on ponds inevitably interbreed with wild mallards. Breeding season is in mid-April. A clutch consists of 8 to 14

white, brownish, or pale green eggs, which are incubated 26 to 28 days. The birds reach sexual maturity toward the end of their first year.

Northern Pintail
Anas acuta

Size: 25½ inches (65 cm)

Origin: Northern and central Eurasia; North America.

Description: Pintails are large, slender, long-necked birds. The drake is dove gray with a brown head and a white throat and breast. The white extends up the side of the head in a stripe that ends at eye height. The undertail coverts and the long, narrow, pointed tail are black. The bill and the legs are bluish gray. The female is brown and can be distinguished from other female dabbling ducks by her long, thin neck and pointed tail.

Northern pintails breed easily. Females lay a clutch of 7 to 11 cream-colored eggs, which take about 22 days to hatch.

Habitat: Large lakes with plenty of vegetation in open, treeless landscapes. Migratory birds in their lands of origin.

Captivity: The pintail is an elegant ornamental duck. It is lively, peaceful, winter hardy, and modest in its demands. Pintails have lived in captivity up to 20 years.

Breeding: Breeding pintails on largish ponds surrounded by dense vegetation is quite easy. These ducks nest hidden in tall grass and other leafy plants, and they also accept nest houses and boxes. The breeding season starts in mid-April. A clutch consists of 7 to 11 cream-colored to greenish yellow eggs, which are incubated from 21 to 23 days. Raising the ducklings presents no problems. The young are ready to fly at seven weeks and reach sexual maturity by the end of the year. They often do not breed until the second year.

Gadwall

Anas strepera

Size: 19¾ inches (50 cm)

Origin: Central Eurasia; North America.

Description: The gadwall is somewhat smaller than the mallard. The drake is gray all over except for the black tail coverts and some chestnut brown on the inner wing. The bill is gray; the legs, orange-yellow. Females are predominantly brown and can be distinguished from female mallards by their yellow bills with a gray center ridge and by the white speculum.

Habitat: Large, shallow, inland waters with lush vegetation offering a plentiful food supply. Not in wooded areas. Migratory birds in their lands of origin.

Captivity: The gadwall is an attractively colored duck that is gregarious and modest in its demands. Since it is migratory, it cannot winter over outside. It feeds primarily on vegetable matter. If a pair with trimmed wings is released on the right kind of pond or lake, the birds may settle there. Gadwalls are faithful to their nest sites and will return there the following spring with their grown young. In captivity, gadwalls can live up to 16 or 17 years.

Breeding: Breeding gadwalls is not difficult if they have a pond that is surrounded by grass and low shrubbery. They nest in dense vegetation. The breeding season runs from late April to early May. A clutch consists of 8 to 12 cream-colored eggs, which are incubated 25 to 27

Falcated teals like to nest among bushes near water and will breed in well-planted garden ponds.

days. Raising the ducklings is unproblematic. The young ducks are able to fly at seven weeks and reach sexual maturity toward the end of their first year.

Falcated Teal
Anas falcata

Size: 19 inches

Origin: From central Siberia to northern Japan.

Description: Falcated teals are smaller than mallards. The drake has a purplish chestnut crown and iridescent copper- to bronze-colored plumage on the front of the head and the cheeks. A broad green band reaches from the eyes to the long crest at the back of the head. The throat is white with a black collar running across the white. The back and the breast have white feathers with black edges forming a scallop pattern. The wing coverts are light gray with white tips. Long, crescent-shaped, black-and-white extended secondary feathers curve down over the hind parts on both sides of the tail. The undertail coverts are black with a large, bold, creamy yellow patch on each side. The flanks and abdomen have fine black-and-white barring. The female resembles the female mallard but has a short, thick crest.

Habitat: Bogs and swampy rivers running through forests. In the winter, falcated teals are found in rice fields and on inland lakes. Migratory birds in their lands of origin.

Captivity: This is a very decorative duck that is gregarious, modest in its demands, and winter hardy. It feeds primarily on vegetable matter. If several drakes are kept, they engage in communal courtship displays in the

Male northern shovelers are one of the most colorful ornamental ducks.

presence of the females, which take active parts in the displays.

Breeding: Breeding these ducks is not difficult because at this time only birds bred in captivity are available for sale. They will breed even in garden ponds if these are well planted. The nest is built among bushes not too far from the water. Falcated teals do not accept nest houses or nest baskets. Between mid-May and mid-June, 6 to 10 brownish yellow eggs are laid and incubated for 25 to 26 days. The young ducks usually start breeding when barely one year old.

Northern Shoveler, Common Shoveler, European Shoveler

Anas clypeata

Size: 19¾ inches (50 cm)

Origin: Northern and central Eurasia; North America.

Description: Shovelers are the only ducks with a huge spatulate bill.

The drake has a bottle-green head, a white breast, light blue inner wings, a large white area on the shoulders, and bright chestnut underparts. The bill is black and the legs orange-yellow. The female is brown but can be easily distinguished from other species by her large spoon-shaped bill.

Notice the size of the bill on this female northern shoveler. Shovelers are noted for their spatulate bills, which are larger than those of any other member of the duck family.

Habitat: Shallow water with lush vegetation offering plenty of food. Migratory birds in their lands of origin.

Captivity: A drake in his nuptial plumage is the most colorful ornamental duck and a very handsome bird. These ducks have peaceful dispositions, but they cannot winter where it gets very cold because the lamellae of their bills ice over when the temperature drops too low. Shovelers have special nutritional demands. With their bills, which are used like sieves, they strain out plankton from the water's surface. Typically, several drakes form a "convoy," swimming close together behind the other and incessantly skimming the water. These ducks need diets high in protein. They can live up to 19 years in captivity.

Breeding: Breeding shovelers is not difficult if you have a pond for them that is surrounded by thick grass, leafy plants, and bushes. These birds breed from early April to June. A clutch consists of 8 to 12 grayish green or, more rarely, cream-colored eggs. Incubation lasts 25 to 27 days. Popular rearing foods are starter meal for turkeys, duckweed, and mosquito larvae. Northern shovelers reach sexual maturity at 10 to 11 months of age but don't breed until their second year.

European Wigeon
Anas penelope

Size: 17¾ inches (45 cm)
Origin: Northern Eurasia.
Description: The drake has a chestnut brown head with a yellow

The European or Eurasian wigeon is a strict vegetarian, so be sure to provide this species with grass for grazing.

blaze on the forehead. The body is gray with a white abdomen and black undertail coverts. The breast is a pinkish wine red. The bill is lead gray; the legs, black. The female differs from other ornamental species by her round head, small bill, and the reddish brown color of her plumage.

Habitat: Shallow water with lush vegetation. Often found on bits of open water in marshy meadows of the Arctic tundra. Winters along ice-free ocean bays. Migratory birds in their lands of origin.

Captivity: The European wigeon is a decorative ornamental duck that is winter hardy, modest in its demands, and gregarious. Its call is a two-syllable whistle that sounds like "wa'-chew." The whistle accounts for the German name for wigeons, which is *pfeifente,* or whistling duck. European wigeons are pure vegetari-

The American wigeon has been called the baldpate because of its white head feathers.

ans, and they need grass to graze on. The highest age reached by this duck species in captivity is 24 years.

Breeding: It is possible to breed this species on a garden pond that is surrounded by bushes and other vegetation if there is also a lawn or

Female American wigeons do not like to be disturbed while they are incubating their eggs.

meadow nearby. The nest is built in shrubbery or in a nest house. The breeding season is from mid-May to early June. The clutch usually consists of 9 creamy yellow eggs that are incubated 22 to 25 days by the female. Rearing the ducklings presents no problems since they start to forage very early. The ducklings are able to fly at six weeks of age and may reach sexual maturity at ten months of age, although most mature a bit later.

American Wigeon (Baldpate)
Anas americana

Size: 18 to 22¾ inches (46 to 58 cm)

Origin: Alaska, Canada, and the western United States.

Description: The forehead and crown of the drake are white, and a broad streak of green runs from the eyes to the nape. The rest of the head and the upper throat are grayish white, delicately dotted with black. The tertials are long, broad, lance-shaped, black-and-white feathers. The upper parts, breast, and flanks are reddish brown with a white abdomen. There is also a white patch on the side of the rear end, and the tail coverts are black. The female has a mottled brown head, a blue bill with black tip, lance-shaped brown-and-white tertial feathers, and light and dark brown wing and breast feathers.

Habitat: Prairie and tundra lakes and open marshland. In the winter, flooded fields and rice paddies. Migratory birds in their land of origin.

Captivity: Not commonly kept in captivity in North America, but wild birds may visit your duck pond during the year.

Breeding: Nests are built underneath bushes or in nest houses. The female does not tolerate disruptions during incubation. The breeding season runs from May to June, and a clutch of 8 to 10 creamy white eggs hatches after 22 to 25 days of incubation. The ducklings are hardy, grow quickly, and reach sexual maturity at 10 months of age.

Chiloë Wigeon

Anas sibilatrix

Size: 17¾ inches (45 cm)

Origin: From southern Brazil to Tierra del Fuego.

Description: The color pattern of the two sexes is the same. The front of the head from the forehead to the chin is white. There is a whitish ear patch. The crown, sides of the head, and neck are black with an iridescent green sheen. The throat and crop region is barred black and white in a scale pattern. The tertials are broad, lance-shaped, and black with white edges. The wing coverts have a large white area, and the speculum is a velvety black with a metallic green sheen. The flanks are orange-brown; the abdomen and tail coverts, white; and the tail, black. The bill and the legs are lead gray.

Habitat: Shallow lakes and swamps in the pampas region. Migratory birds in their lands of origin.

Captivity: This species is highly recommended as an ornamental duck. It is gregarious, has modest demands, and is winter hardy. Both sexes wear their colorful nuptial plumage all year-round. These ducks can be kept even on small garden ponds, but they do need a grassy area for grazing.

Unlike many other duck species, male and female Chiloë wigeons have the same color patterns.

Female green-winged teals lay clutches of 6 to 12 eggs. The ducklings can be sensitive to cold and moisture, so they are best brooded and hatched in an incubator.

Breeding: Chiloë wigeons are easy to breed. Set up brood houses close to the water. The drake keeps guard over the sitting female. The breeding season starts in early April. A clutch of 6 to 11 off-white eggs hatches after 24 to 25 days of incubation. The ducklings are very independent and immediately start foraging. Both parents share in the care of the young, which is very unusual for dabbling ducks. Unattached drakes readily accept orphaned ducklings of other species and act as model parents for them. Young ducks acquire their adult plumage in the fall of their first year. They are sometimes ready to breed at the end of their first year but more

often not until the spring of their second year.

European Green-Winged Teal
Anas crecca

Size: 13¾ inches (35 cm)

Origin: Northern and central Eurasia; also North America. The male of the North American subspecies has a white mark on the side of the breast.

Description: The green-winged teal is the smallest wild duck of the northern hemisphere. The head of the drake is chestnut brown with a broad green band running from the eye across the side of the face to the nape. Most of the rest of the plumage is delicately barred black and white, and the breast is yellow-

Male green-winged teals engage in communal courtship displays during mating season.

ish white with black spots. There is a large creamy yellow patch bordered with black on the side of the rear end and a white shoulder stripe. The speculum is green. The female is mottled brown and buff with light-colored cheeks and underparts and a green speculum.

Habitat: Shallow inland waters with lush vegetation; also lakes in marsh areas and heaths. Migratory birds.

Captivity: This decorative duck is recommended for an aviary and garden pond. It is gregarious, modest in its demands, and winter hardy. Males engage in interesting communal courtship displays during which they utter the "krick" whistle. Two banded wild green-winged teal are known to have reached 17 years of age.

Breeding: Breeding these ducks in captivity is easy. They build nests in thick grass or other leafy plants and also accept nest boxes. The breeding season is in early May. A clutch of 6 to 12 cream-colored

eggs is incubated 21 to 25 days. The ducklings are rather delicate and sensitive to cold and moisture. They should therefore be reared artificially in a brooder. They are able to fly at 44 days of age and ready to breed at the end of their first year.

Garganey (Cricket Teal)
Anas querquedula
    Size: 15 inches (35 cm)
    Origin: Central Eurasia.
    Description: The drake has a brown head and neck with a broad white band running from the eye to the nape. The brass-brown breast is sharply set off from the gray flanks, which are delicately barred with black. Long black-and-white scapulars hang down over the green speculum. The female resembles the female green-winged teal, but the colors on the head show greater contrast, and the speculum is blue.

    Habitat: Shallow inland waters with lush vegetation offering plenty of food. Migratory birds.

Captivity: This duck with its rather subdued but attractive coloring is well suited to being kept in an aviary or on a garden pond. It is gregarious and modest in its demands but not quite winter hardy. Wild garganeys live up to eight years.

Breeding: Garganeys are easy to breed on a small garden pond surrounded by dense vegetation. The breeding season is from mid-April to May. A clutch of 8 to 11 creamy yellow eggs is incubated 21 to 23 days. The females are reliable brooders and good mothers. The ducklings are able to fly at five to six weeks of age, and they reach sexual maturity at ten months, although they usually don't breed until their second year.

Cinnamon Teal
Anas cyanoptera

Size: 14½ to 17 inches (37 to 43 cm)

Origin: Western North America; northwestern and southern South America.

Description: The drake is a deep chestnut brown with light blue inner wings, a green speculum, black tail coverts, a black bill, and orange-yellow legs. The female is brown with light blue inner wings and a green speculum.

Habitat: Shallow ponds with lots of vegetation, grassy marshes; in winter, lagoons and rice paddies. Migratory birds.

Captivity: This is an attractive and quiet duck suitable for an aviary or garden pond, but it sometimes does not get along well with other ducks; it is not winter hardy and therefore needs a shelter.

Breeding: Breeding attempts in aviaries and on backyard ponds are often successful. The breeding season is from mid-April to late May. During this period, breeding pairs cannot be kept together with others of their species or with any other small ducks, such as blue-winged teals, green-winged teals, or garganeys, because the drakes are extremely aggressive. Nests are built in dense vegetation. A clutch consists of 10 to 12 white to yellowish eggs, which are incubated for 24 to 25 days. Rearing the ducklings is unproblematic. The young ducks are able to fly at about seven weeks of age and reach sexual maturity toward the end of the year.

Baikal Teal, Formosa Teal, Spectacled Teal
Anas formosa

Size: 15¾ inches (40 cm)

Origin: Northeastern Siberia; winters in China and Japan.

Description: The head of the drake is black at the top. The dark yellow face has a crescent-shaped stripe starting behind the eye and running down the side of the neck. A black line cuts downward across the yellow cheek and curves forward, ending in a black area on the chin and throat. The breast is a pale wine red with dark round spots, and the flanks are gray with delicate, wavy barring. The elongated, narrow scapulars taper to a point and are black along the center, yellow along the upper edge, and brown along the lower edge. The speculum is a bronze green. The female resembles the female green-winged teal but has a white spot at the base of the bill.

Habitat: Ponds and rivers in the forests of the Siberian taiga. The Baikal teal is migratory, wintering over on the flooded rice paddies of China and Japan.

Captivity: This is a lovely, small ornamental duck that is easy to keep, gregarious, and winter hardy. Birds reared in captivity in Europe are quite tame and calm. If several drakes live together, they engage in communal courtship displays in the spring.

Breeding: Offspring cannot regularly be expected, but breeding efforts on garden ponds have sometimes been successful. The nest is built on the cover of grass or other leafy plants, always close to the ground but on dry ground. They will also use a concealed ground-level nest box. The breeding season is from the end of April to early July. A clutch of 6 to 9 grayish green eggs is incubated for 23 to 26 days. Rearing the ducklings is unproblematic. They are able to fly after 46 days and reach sexual maturity toward the end of their first year.

Blue-Winged Teal
Anas discors

Size: 14½ to 16 inches (37 to 41 cm)

Origin: Across the middle of North America.

Description: The head of the drake is bluish gray with a black

The male blue-winged teal has a bluish gray head with black feathers on the crown, forehead, and chin.

The female blue-winged teal is less brightly colored than the male. Her head feathers are brown and she lacks the black crown, forehead, and chin feathers.

crown, forehead, and chin, and a bold white crescent starting above the eye and running down to the chin. The inner wing is powder blue; the speculum is green. The underparts are dark yellow densely covered with round black spots, and there is a white patch on the rear flank. The bill is black and the legs, yellow. The female is brown with pale blue inner wings and a white abdomen.

Habitat: Shallow lakes that offer plenty of food; ponds with good landing sites; marshlands. Migratory birds.

Captivity: This is an attractively colored small duck that is gregarious and easy to keep. It is ideal both for an aviary and for a garden pond, but it is not quite winter hardy and needs a shelter for the cold season.

Breeding: Breeding this species presents no great problems. The nest is built close to the water but on dry ground and is well hidden in dense vegetation. The breeding season is from late May to early June. A clutch of 7 to 10 white eggs is incubated in 24 to 26 days. The ducklings are at first very shy. They are also sensitive to cold and dampness. The young birds are able to fly at about six weeks of age and reach breeding age in about ten months. If blue-winged and cinnamon teal are kept together, they often form mixed pairs.

Silver Teal
Anas versicolor

Size: 17 to 19 inches (43 to 48 cm)

Origin: In South America from Bolivia to the southern tip of Argentina; Falkland Islands.

Description: The two sexes are very similar. The crown is dark brown down to the eyes, as is the back of the neck and the nape. The rest of the head is cream colored. The breast and abdomen are a muddy yellow, densely dotted with dark brown. This pattern gradually changes to fine, dark brown barring on the sides of the abdomen and on the flanks. The upper parts are dark brown with a brown scallop pattern on the upper back. The speculum is an iridescent blue-green bordered on both sides by white. The lower back down to the tail coverts shows a delicate black-and-white barring. The bill is pale blue with a black ridge and an orange-yellow spot at the base. The legs are gray. The female is slightly smaller, and the color contrasts on the head are less strong.

Habitat: Shallow lakes with plentiful food supply, especially in the pampas region of Argentina.

Captivity: This is a handsomely colored small duck that is well suited for a garden pond or an aviary with a pond. It is gregarious, modest in its demands, and almost winter hardy. Its nutritional demands are the same as those of other small ducks.

Breeding: Breeding this duck is not difficult. The breeding season starts in mid-April. The nest is built on dry ground in tall grass or other leafy plants. A clutch of 7 to 10 mud-yellow eggs is incubated for 24 to 26 days. It is best to rear the ducklings in a brooder. The young ducks are sexually mature by the end of their first year but usually don't breed until their second year.

Ringed Teal
Callonetta leucophrys

Size: 13¾ inches (35 cm)

Origin: From southern Brazil and southeastern Bolivia to Argentina.

Description: The drake has a black crown and nape; the rest of the head is off-white with delicate black shading. The mantle is grayish brown; the scapulars are bright chestnut red; and the back, rump, and tail are black with a metallic green sheen. The wings are black with a large white patch on the wing coverts and a bronzish green speculum. The breast is pink with round, black dots. The flanks and abdomen are gray with delicate black barring, and the undertail coverts are black with a white spot on the side. The bill is bluish gray; the legs, pink. The female has a dark brown crown and a band of the same color below the eyes. The sides of the head are white with a light brown spot on the cheek. The shoulders are a muddy brown instead of the chestnut red found on the male. The underparts are a dirty white with broad brown crossbarring.

Habitat: Puddles and swamps in the light tropical forests that form the transition between rain forest and pampas.

Captivity: The ringed teal is an attractively colored small ornamental duck that is lively and gregarious. It is not winter hardy and has to be kept at temperatures above freezing to keep it from losing its toes to frostbite. This duck should be kept only in aviaries and without curtailing its flying capacities. It likes to feed on soaked dried shrimp and small grains such as millet or canary seed. In addition, it should receive high-protein pellets.

Breeding: This species nests in tree holes and needs nest boxes that are mounted well above ground. The breeding season starts at the end of May. A clutch of 4 to 8 white eggs is incubated for 23 days. Letting the natural mother rear the young has shown the best results. The ducklings need lots of warmth. Both parents share equally in the rearing of their offspring.

Bahama Pintail, White-Cheeked Pintail, or Summer Duck
Anas bahamensis
Size: 13¾ to 15 inches (35 to 38 cm)

Origin: Caribbean islands, South America, and the Galapagos Islands.

Description: Both sexes look alike. The cheeks, throat, and front of the neck are white; the rest of the plumage is yellowish brown with black markings. The speculum is an iridescent green. The pointed tail is light cinnamon in color. The bill is blue with a red patch at the base, and the legs are lead gray.

Habitat: Puddles with plenty of vegetation, mangrove swamps, lagoons along the coast. Resident birds.

Captivity: This attractively colored, small tropical duck is gregarious and modest in its demands, but it is not winter hardy. It is well suited for an aviary or a small garden pond.

Breeding: This species is easy to breed and likes nest boxes best. Its breeding season can begin anywhere from February to June, depending on the amount of rainfall and the availability of food. A clutch consists of 8 to 12 mud-colored eggs that are incubated for 25 to 26

The Bahama pintail is sometimes called the white-cheeked pintail for obvious reasons. These birds are not acclimated to cold temperatures, so provide them with shelter during wintertime.

days. The female is a reliable brooder and rears the ducklings by herself. The young are ready to fly at six to seven weeks of age. They reach sexual maturity at the end of the first year but don't start breeding until the second year.

Mandarin Duck

Aix galericulata

Size: 17 inches (43 cm)

Origin: The Far East; introduced into southern England.

Description: The drake is very striking with dramatic color contrasts on the head, a crest of long feathers on the nape, small orange

"wing sails" on the back, a red bill, and yellow legs. The female is inconspicuous, having grayish brown upper parts, marbled light underparts, and a white line running from the eye to the nape. Her bill is gray.

Habitat: Ponds, lakes, and slow-moving rivers in deciduous forests, none of them with abundant food sources; also, mountain lakes in evergreen forests. Migratory birds.

Captivity: The mandarin duck is one of the most spectacular small ornamental ducks and is reminiscent of Chinese and Japanese paintings. Since it is winter hardy and has modest nutritional demands, it is an ideal duck for garden ponds there as well as for aviaries. If kept on waters in well-wooded parks, mandarin ducks don't need to have their flying powers restrained. If you want to keep the ducks from migrating in the winter, they have to have open water and sufficient food. If mandarin ducks are kept together with other

The mandarin duck is ideal for garden ponds or aviaries.

The male mandarin duck is one of the most spectacularly marked ducks. Mandarin ducks are hole nesters that require nest boxes for breeding success.

ducks, the drakes unfortunately have a tendency to be aggressive and to pursue and rape females. During the breeding season in the spring, the drakes perform impressive communal courtship displays. This species likes to feed on tender plant material and can jump 3 feet (91 cm) straight up in the air in order to reach tempting greenery.

Breeding: Breeding mandarin ducks is easy. They are pure hole nesters that never build nests in the open and always require nest boxes. In their native habitat, they use tree holes made by woodpeckers and hollow tree sections that are often 30 to 60 feet (10 to 20 m) off the ground. If you keep these ducks on a garden pond or in an aviary, the nest boxes

should be 20 inches (50 cm) above the ground, and a small ladder should lead up to the entry hole so that birds with clipped wings can get to the nest. Since female mandarin ducks do not pluck breast feathers to line the nest, the bottom of the nest cavity should be covered with sawdust, peat moss, or dry leaves. The breeding season is from late April to early May. A clutch of 8 to 12 creamy white eggs is incubated for 31 days. The newly hatched ducklings climb up the vertical walls of the nest cavity, using their needle-sharp claws, and then drop to the ground, where the mother waits for them and leads them to the water in a group. Since the ducklings weigh less than an ounce (25 g) and their bones are

Here you can see the differences in plumage and coloration between the male (left) and female (right) wood duck.

still soft and elastic, they land on the forest floor from heights of 50 to 60 feet (15 to 18 m) with no harm. The ducklings are able to fly after 63 days. The young males acquire their nuptial plumage in the fall of their first year, and the females lay eggs after one year. Usually, however, the eggs are not fertile until the end of the second year. Female mandarin ducks and female wood ducks look rather

During courtship, a male wood duck may offer his mate food tidbits, which is a highly unusual duck behavior.

similar, and if both species are kept together, crossbreeding is common. The offspring, however, are always infertile.

Wood Duck (Carolina Duck)
Aix sponsa

Size: 17 to 20 inches (43 to 51 cm)

Origin: Eastern North America, Cuba.

Description: The drake is brightly colored above, with a long, curving crest, a bold white chin spot, and a red bill. The legs are yellow. The female has a gray crest and a wide, white eye ring that extends in a pointed line behind the eye. Otherwise, she closely resembles the female mandarin duck.

Habitat: Small ponds and rivers in wooded country. Visits freshwater marshes in the late summer and fall. In northern breeding areas, wood ducks are migratory.

Captivity: This duck is hardly less spectacular than the mandarin duck. Like the latter, it is winter hardy and has modest demands. And it is less aggressive. Wood ducks do not engage in communal courtship displays, but the courtship ritual with which the drake woos his mate is quite striking. He sometimes even offers her tidbits of food, a courtship display that is extremely rare in ducks. Wood ducks are quite friendly toward their caretakers, but if they are not fenced, they can do considerable damage to young plants in a garden. Wood ducks are not as well suited to flying freely in large parks as mandarin ducks, because they often migrate to warmer climates in the fall and fail to return in the spring. Crossbreeding with many other species of ornamental ducks is common. Unfortunately, the coloring of hybrid offspring is always much duller than that of normal wood duck drakes.

Breeding: Breeding wood ducks in captivity is often successful. The breeding season starts in April. Wood ducks are hole nesters that brood in tree holes, and their needs are the same as those of mandarin ducks. A clutch consists of 15 creamy white eggs, which are incubated for 28 to 32 days. If the eggs are removed, a duck may lay up to 30 eggs in a breeding season. These eggs can be given to a call duck for brooding, or they can be artificially incubated. The ducklings can easily climb up on vertical wire mesh with their sharp claws, and their rearing cages, therefore, have to be enclosed with wire mesh at the top, too. The ducklings are independent

at six weeks of age and are able to fly at nine weeks of age.

By the time they are four and one half months old, young wood ducks resemble adult birds. The females already lay fertile eggs when they are one year old.

Ornamental Ducks: Diving Ducks

Diving ducks swim with their bodies lower in the water than dabbling ducks, and their legs are set farther back on the body, close to the tail end. They dive with a quick jerk and feed at the bottom, often many feet below the water's surface.

Red-Crested Pochard
Netta rufina
   Size: 21¾ inches (55 cm)
   Origin: From central Eurasia eastward to western Siberia.

Male red-crested pochards are peaceful birds except in the spring, when they become aggressive.

Female red-crested pochards are less brightly colored than the males.

Description: The drake has a bushy, erect, golden orange crest, and the rest of the head and upper neck are fox red. The lower neck and breast are black. The flanks, a band on the shoulder, and the underside of the wings are white. The bill, eyes, and feet are red. The female is brown with conspicuously light cheeks.

Habitat: Large, warm, shallow lakes and ponds with lush vegetation. Migratory birds.

Captivity: The red-crested pochard is very decorative, modest in its demands, and winter hardy. In the spring, five or six drakes often perform a communal courtship display. Later, the drake may engage in courtship-feeding of his mate. The drakes are aggressive only in the spring; later, they are peaceful. Red-crested pochards are vegetarians and have many traits in common with dabbling ducks, such as cropping the grass in a meadow. If they are kept on a small garden pond, they should, if possible, not be combined with other species. Red-crested pochards can live up to 15 years in captivity.

Keep red-crested pochard ducklings away from young birds of other species because the young pochards can be aggressive toward other ducklings.

Breeding: Breeding this species is easy. The ducks accept nest boxes and nest houses, and the drake keeps guard near the nest. The eggs are laid in early May. They are grayish yellow, and there are between 6 and 12 in a clutch, which is incubated 26 to 28 days. The ducklings are aggressive and rough with ducklings of other species. Rearing them presents no problems, especially if their diets are supplemented with duckweed. They are able to fly at 26 to 27 days of age and reach sexual maturity toward the end of the year.

Rosy-Bill
Netta peposaca
   Size: 22¾ inches (58 cm)
   Origin: Southern South America.
   Description: The drake keeps his nuptial plumage all year. His head, neck, and breast are black with a purple sheen; the upper parts are black and the underparts gray. The bill and a nublike enlargement at its base are a bright pink to red. The eyes are orange-red, and the legs are yellowish. The female can be distinguished from a female red-crested pochard by her overall dark brown coloring and her whitish chin.
   Habitat: Small, shallow lakes with plenty of vegetation in the pampas, lakes with reedy shores near the coast. Migratory birds.
   Captivity: This is a decorative species that is peaceable, modest in its demands, and winter hardy. A single pair can be kept on a small garden pond, but larger ponds are a better environment for them. Rosy-bills, which are largely vegetarian, graze on meadows and like tender young plant parts. It is therefore not advisable to let them run loose near your flowerbeds. Rosy-bills tend to interbreed with red-crested pochards and other diving ducks.
   Breeding: Breeding rosy-bills is easy. They nest on dry ground among grass and other leafy plants, but they also accept nest boxes and nest houses. Egg laying starts in mid-May. A clutch consists of 10 to 12 grayish green eggs, which are incubated 27 to 29 days. The females are reliable brooders and excellent mothers. The ducklings are robust and easy to rear. The young drakes get their adult plumage toward the end of their first year, but the females don't start laying until they are almost two years old.

European Pochard
Aythya ferina
   Size: 17¾ inches (45 cm)
   Origin: Northern Eurasia from Great Britain eastward to Mongolia.
   Description: The head and neck of the European pochard are chestnut red; the back and flanks, light gray; and the breast and tail feathers, black. The bill is grayish blue with black at the base and tip. The eyes are red; the legs, dark gray. The female is grayish brown with a darker brown head, neck, and breast.
   Habitat: Reedy inland waters with plenty of food. Migratory birds.
   Captivity: This decorative duck, which is gregarious, modest in its

demands, and winter hardy, should be kept only on larger bodies of water, not on small garden ponds or in swimming basins of aviaries. It needs water of at least 28 inches (70 cm) deep for diving. European pochards can live 20 to 22 years in captivity.

Breeding: Breeding European pochards is possible only in large park ponds. The breeding season is in May and June. Nests are built amid leafy vegetation or in reeds, but nest houses and nest boxes are accepted, too. A clutch consists of 8 to 11 grayish green eggs and is incubated for 24 to 26 days. The females are reliable brooders and good mothers. Rearing these ducklings presents no problems, especially if duckweed is available. The ducklings are able to fly at 55 days of age and reach sexual maturity toward the end of their first year.

Tufted Duck
Aythya fuligula

Size: 17 inches (43 cm)

Origin: Northern Eurasia and eastward to the Pacific Ocean.

Description: The drake is primarily black above with a pointed crest on the back of the head, which has a purple tinge. The eyes are light yellow; the flanks and abdomen, white. The bill is bluish gray, and the legs are lead gray. The female is almost a uniform blackish brown with only the hint of a crest.

Habitat: Large, still, or slow-moving waters with small islands and lush vegetation along the shores. On waters that stay open during the winter, tufted ducks are resident.

Captivity: This species is decorative, lively, peaceful, modest in its demands, and winter hardy, but it can be kept only on larger ponds and needs at least 28 inches (70 cm) of water for diving. It feeds primarily on mollusks, which it dives up to 40 feet (12 m) to find. Tufted ducks can live 18 years or more in captivity.

Breeding: Attempts to breed tufted ducks are not always successful. The breeding season is from mid-May to mid-June. This duck accepts nest boxes only reluctantly and prefers to build her nest hidden in dense vegetation close to the water. A clutch consists of 8 to 10 grayish green eggs, which are incubated 23 to 25 days. The ducklings are independent after just a few days and pay little attention to their mother from that point on. They are able to fly at eight to nine weeks of age and grow their adult plumage during the first fall. Successful breeding, however, is not likely until the second year.

Ruddy Duck (North American Ruddy Duck)
Oxyura jamaicensis

Size: 14½ to 16 inches (37 to 41 cm)

Origin: Western and central North America; Central America; from northwestern South America south as far as Tierra del Fuego.

Description: The drake has a black head and neck, white cheeks, and a pale blue bill. The breast, back,

The male ruddy duck is distinguished by his unusual light blue bill.

does not like to leave the water, place food dishes at the water's edge, or offer grains such as millet, wheat, and barley on the water. Duckweed is very popular with ruddy ducks.

Breeding: Breeding ruddy ducks is not difficult. Offer nest sites in the form of a hollow in the ground that is filled with dry leaves, or a flat fruit crate placed among vegetation right next to the water. The breeding season begins in mid-May. A clutch consists of 6 to 12 very large, whitish eggs with thick shells. Incubation lasts 23 to 26 days. The big, strong ducklings are led first by both parents, then later by the mother only. They are able to fly at 52 to 60 days of age and are ready to breed between 10 and 12 months of age.

and flanks are chestnut red; the abdomen, a muddy brown mixed with white; the undertail coverts, white; the pointed tail, grayish brown; and the legs, dark blue. The female is brownish gray with a dark brown crown and a stripe of the same color crossing the light cheek from the base of the lower mandible to the ear region. The bill and the legs are dark grayish blue.

Habitat: Shallow waters with lush vegetation offering plenty of food. Migratory in the northern areas of distribution.

Captivity: This is a charming small diving duck, gregarious, lively, winter hardy, and modest in its food demands. Ruddy ducks have been bred in captivity with some frequency in recent years and are often available for sale. Since this species

Common Goldeneye (European Goldeneye)
Bucephala clangula

Size: 18 inches (46 cm)

Origin: Northern Eurasia and North America.

Description: The drake has a large, almost triangular, greenish black head with a large white spot beside the black bill and below the light yellow eye. The upper parts are black except for the scapulars, which are white with diagonal black lines. The underparts are white, and the legs are yellow. The female is smaller than the male and has a brown head, a white neck ring, and a grayish brown body.

Habitat: Large ponds with clear water. Migratory birds.

The common goldeneye is an attractive, lively diving duck that nests in trees.

Captivity: This attractive and lively diving duck sometimes teases other kinds of ducks but never harms them. The drake engages in complex courtship displays, during which the head is tossed back onto the rump. These ducks need food that is high in animal proteins, such as shrimp, pieces of fish, and ground meat. In addition, they should be fed wheat grain, turkey pellets, and finely chopped greens. Common goldeneyes can live 15 to 20 years in captivity. They are winter hardy.

Breeding: Goldeneyes can be bred only on largish ponds or on garden ponds with clear clean water. A breeding pair should be kept by itself. The breeding season is from mid-March to early May. A clutch consists of 8 to 10 bluish green eggs, which are incubated 27 to 32 days. Goldeneyes brood their eggs only in nest boxes that are suspended above ground. The duck-lings leave the nest hole by letting themselves drop to the ground. If they are reared artificially, they easily climb up the walls of boxes or on wire mesh by using their sharp claws. Rearing them is not altogether simple. They need a ration high in protein. A starter diet made up of starter ration for duck or turkey chicks, cooked and ground beef heart, dry cottage cheese, duckweed, mosquito larvae, and mealworms is recommended. The ducklings are able to fly at eight weeks of age and reach sexual maturity at two years of age. Successful breeding results cannot be expected until the third year.

Showing Utility Ducks

The breeds listed below are eligible to be shown in APA–sanctioned shows. Descriptions of the birds will be listed alphabetically by weight class as determined by the APA. The APA recognized the following duck breeds in late 2004:

Heavyweight Class: Pekin, Aylesbury, Rouen, Muscovy, Appleyard, Saxony

Medium-weight Class: Cayuga, Crested, Swedish, Buff

Lightweight Class: Runner, Campbell, Magpie, Welsh Harlequin

Bantamweight Class: Call, East Indie, Mallard (which is listed in this book at the beginning of the ornamental duck section)

We will also look at a few American duck breeds that the APA has yet to sanction, such as the Ancona and the Australian Spotted.

Utility Ducks: Heavyweight Breeds

Aylesbury Duck

Weight of drake: 7¾ pounds (3.5 kg)

Weight of female: 6½ pounds (3 kg)

Origin: This breed was developed in England as a market duck.

Description: This is a deep-bodied but not plump-looking white duck with horizontal carriage.

Eggs: White to greenish. Minimum weight: 2.8 ounces (80 g). Annual production: up to 100 eggs.

Special remarks: In terms of size and heaviness, this is probably the best commercial duck. Its meat is tender, white, and exceptionally tasty. For best development, this

duck needs to be able to run free and should have a place to swim.

Muscovy Duck

Weight of drake: 8¼ pounds (4 kg)

Weight of female: 6½ pounds (3 kg)

Origin: This strain was originally domesticated from the wild muscovy duck (*Cairina moschata*) by the Indians in the rain forests of South America. It was brought to Europe by the Spaniards.

Description: This is a large duck with big red caruncles on the face. The long, very broad body is carried horizontally. It is broad but not very deep, and there is no keel formation. The tail is long. In the wild form, both sexes are black with a green and blue luster and white wing coverts. Color varieties include white, blue, chocolate, pastel, and silver.

Eggs: White, often with a yellow tinge. Minimum weight: 2.5 ounces (70 g). Annual production: 80 to 100 eggs.

The muscovy duck was domesticated by native peoples of South America and brought to Europe by Spanish explorers.

The Pekin duck is commonly raised for both eggs and meat. It was developed by crossing European and Chinese breeding stock.

Special remarks: Muscovies are fed and maintained like other domestic ducks. They like to graze and are somewhat sensitive to the cold. They are good fliers and brood two to three times a year in nest boxes hung high. Nest boxes set up inside shelters should be raised, too. Indoors, muscovies start laying as early as January or February; outdoors, somewhat later. The ducks brood and rear their young reliably, and therefore they also make good foster mothers for ornamental ducklings. The drakes are often aggressive, chase other poultry, and rape other domestic female ducks. Muscovy ducks are excellent meat producers with a high proportion of breast meat. They can also be fattened for market. Young drakes should be butchered at 11 to 12 weeks of age; young females are best at 10 weeks. The meat is darkish but of excellent taste. Muscovies can be crossed with other domestic ducks. The offspring are not fertile but have good meat.

Pekin Duck

Weight of drake: 7¾ pounds (3.5 kg)

Weight of female: 6½ pounds (3 kg)

Origin: This breed was developed in the United States around 1870 by crossing Aylesbury ducks with stock of Chinese origin. In Europe, Pekin ducks have been bred since the beginning of the 20th century.

Description: This duck has a deep body that looks almost like a square with rounded edges. The body is carried with the front slightly raised on legs of medium height. The plumage is pure white.

Eggs: White to yellowish. Minimum weight: 2.5 ounces (70 g). Annual production: 100 to 130 eggs.

Special remarks: This is the most common commercial duck raised for both meat and eggs. Its ratio of converting feed into meat is very high, and no other breed grows faster. Eight-week-old ducklings weigh 2½ to 5½ pounds (1 to 2.5 kg) if fed properly. Pekin ducks can be kept relatively closely confined and without swimming water.

Rouen Duck

Weight of drake: 7¾ pounds (3.5 kg)

Weight of female: 6½ pounds (3 kg)

Origin: This duck was originally developed in the Rouen area of France from local farm ducks. The breed's present size and coloring are the result of selective breeding in England. The Rouen duck was introduced into Germany around 1850.

Description: The Rouen duck is a beautifully colored and nobly shaped large duck with a calm nature. It embodies the square shape that breeders of meat ducks aim for. The recognized color strains are "wild," which is equivalent to the natural coloring of the mallard duck, and "blue wild," in which the parts that are black in the "wild strain" are blue.

Eggs: Green, sometimes lighter (whitish) or darker (bluish). Minimum weight: 2.6 ounces (80 g). Annual production: 60 to 90 eggs.

Special remarks: Rouen ducks have a calm temperament and become quite tame. They can be kept successfully in a relatively small space without swimming opportunity. When raised for market, they can reach a weight of 11 pounds (5 kg). The meat is somewhat darker than that of the previously described breeds, but it has an excellent flavor and is tender and juicy. The Rouen is not a good laying duck, and raising Rouen ducklings requires a little more effort during the first few weeks than raising other breeds. The duck-

The "wild" color variation of the Rouen duck shows the breed's mallard heritage.

lings have to be protected, especially against getting wet from above (rain).

Saxony Duck

Weight of drake: 7¾ pounds (3.5 kg)

Weight of female: 6½ pounds (2.9 kg)

Origin: This strain was originally developed in Germany in the 1930s and revived in the 1950s by crossing Rouen, German Pekin, and Pommern ducks.

Description: This is a sturdy utility duck with a long, broad body without any keel formation and with an almost horizontal carriage. The drake has a pigeon blue head and neck and an unbroken white neck ring. The breast, lower neck, and shoulders are rusty red. The breast feathers are lightly edged with silver, the rump is pigeon blue, and the wings are flour colored. The female has a dark yellow head, neck, and breast. The wing coverts are cream colored with a slight bluish tinge and a pigeon blue speculum. There is also a light stripe above the eyes and a hint of a neck ring.

Eggs: White. Minimum weight: 2.8 ounces (80 g). Annual production: 100 to 140 eggs.

Special remarks: The Saxony has all the traits of an ideal duck. Its unusual coloring is a challenge to any breeder, and the duck's economic return is significant. The young birds grow fast, and if they are fed for market, they are generally ready for slaughter at 10 weeks. The egg production is also quite impressive.

Silver Appleyard

Weight of drake: 8 pounds (3.6 kg)

Weight of female: 6 pounds (2.7 kg)

Origin: This breed can trace its origins to British breeder Reginald Appleyard, who set out in the 1940s to create "a beautiful breed of duck, with a combination of beauty, size, lots of big white eggs, and a deep, long, wide breast." By the 1960s, the breed had been brought to America, and it was made available to the public in 1984.

Description: The Silver Appleyard is a blocky duck. The male has greenish black head and neck feathers that sometimes begin to stripe as he ages. The male has white-frosted reddish feathers on his breast, shoulders, and sides, with creamy feathers on his underbody and blackish bronze tail feathers. The female has whitish body feathers with gray, brown, fawn, and buff markings.

Eggs: White. Minimum weight: 2½ ounces (66 g). Annual production: 220 to 265 eggs.

Special remarks: Silver Appleyards are versatile birds that are being raised for show, eggs, or meat production. These birds forage actively and have calm dispositions.

Utility Ducks: Medium-weight Breeds

Ancona Duck

Weight of drake: 6½ pounds (2.9 kg)

Weight of female: 6 pounds (2.7 kg)

Origin: The Ancona originated in Great Britain in the early 1900s and probably was developed from runner ducks and an old Belgian breed called the Huttegen duck. It is closely related to the magpie duck.

Description: The Ancona has mottled plumage that is unique among ducks. There is no set design for it. Anconas usually have white necks that arch slightly forward and hold up medium-sized oval heads. Color varieties include black and white, chocolate and white, silver and white, and tricolor.

Eggs: White, cream, or blue. Minimum weight: 2½ ounces (70 g). Annual production: 210 to 280 eggs.

Special remarks: The Ancona is a fast-growing all-purpose duck, good for either egg or meat production. Its high-quality meat is more flavorful and less fatty than that of most Pekin ducks. These birds are hardy and are well suited for situations where they can forage for some of their food, which can also help control garden pests around a backyard pond.

Buff Duck

Weight of drake: 6½ pounds (3 kg)

Weight of female: 5½ pounds (2.5 kg)

Origin: This breed originated in England around 1880. It was originally called the buff Orpington, after the region of England in which it was developed, but it was introduced to the American fancy as the buff in 1914. It is the only duck breed to be named after a color.

Description: This is a lively, medium-heavy duck with a cylindrical body and moderately upright carriage. The drake has a chocolate brown head and neck; the rest of the plumage is a uniform yellowish brown. The female is yellowish brown all over.

Eggs: Pure white to green. Minimum weight: 2.3 ounces (65 g). Annual production: 150 to 180 eggs.

Special remarks: This is one of the best utility ducks, and it can be kept in relatively crowded quarters. Buffs do not need a place to swim, but they do have to be able to bathe. This breed is probably the most modest in its food needs. The meat is very tender and juicy. The buff is also a good laying duck, starting to lay in December and continuing until August. The taste of the eggs is excellent and similar to that of chicken eggs. Ducklings are easy to raise.

Cayuga Duck

Weight of drake: 6½ pounds (3 kg)

Weight of female: 5½ pounds (2.5 kg)

Origin: The breed originated in the United States and is named after Lake Cayuga in New York. It was introduced to Germany via England around 1870.

Description: This is a medium-sized duck with an almost horizontal carriage and a nicely rounded shape. Both sexes are black with a green metallic luster on the head, neck, and back, and with a bright blue speculum.

Eggs: Pure white to dark green. Minimum weight: 2.3 ounces (65 g). Annual production: 70 to 100 eggs.

Special remarks: The Cayuga is a calm, friendly, hardy duck, but it is not suitable for confined quarters. The taste of the meat is similar to many mallards. The carcass is meaty, and the skin is pure white. Raising ducklings is unproblematic.

Crested Duck

Weight of drake: 5½ pounds (2.5 kg)

Weight of female: 4½ pounds (2 kg)

Origin: The crested duck is a mutation of European farm ducks that has been around for centuries.

Description: The crested ducks is a sturdy farm duck (a farm duck is a utility duck of no particular breed) with a ball-shaped crest on the back of the head, a noticeably bent neck, and a horizontal carriage. All colors and markings are recognized. The crest should be of good size and not lopsided or divided.

Eggs: White; rarely greenish. Minimum weight: 2.1 ounces (60 g). Annual production: approximately 120 eggs.

Special remarks: This lively, friendly, and hardy duck is the prototype for Walt Disney's Donald Duck. It needs a place to swim. The ducklings are easy to raise and mature early. The quality of meat is good, and the laying season lasts from January to July.

Swedish Duck

Weight of drake: 8 pounds (3.6 kg)

Weight of female: 6½ pounds (2.9 kg)

Origin: The Swedish duck can trace its origins to Pomerania, a region on the Polish-German border that was part of the kingdom of Sweden in the 1830s, when the breed began to be developed. The breed was introduced in America in 1884.

Description: The Swedish is a blue duck with a white bib, oval head, and stocky body.

Eggs: White, blue, or green. Minimum weight: 2.8 ounces (79 g). Annual production: 100 to 150 eggs.

Special Remarks: The Swedish is a slow-maturing breed that provides succulent meat with a unique flavor that can be credited to the paddock or orchard areas where these ducks often forage. These ducks have calm temperaments and make good pets.

Utility Ducks: Lightweight Breeds

Australian Spotted

Weight of drake: 2.2 pounds (1 kg)

Weight of female: 2 pounds (.9 kg)

Origin: Despite its non-American name, this breed was developed in the United States. Two breeders in Pennsylvania developed it using call, mallard, northern pintail, and an unknown Australian wild breed. It became widely available in the 1990s.

Description: The Australian Spotted has a teardrop-shaped body and centrally located legs that give the duck a nearly horizontal body carriage. Their oval heads are somewhat streamlined. The bird's neck features a white band, and its body is a deep burgundy color. The bird's breast feathers are burgundy with white feathers in the center. The tail is light gray with black feathers underneath. Head coloration of males depends upon the variety, which includes greenhead, bluehead, and silverhead. The greenhead's body, head, and neck are fawn with dark brown spots. The coloration of the bluehead and the silverhead mimic that of the greenhead, except the bluehead has bluish gray spots and the silverhead has silver spots.

Eggs: Cream, blue, or green. Minimum weight: 1.8 ounces (50.4 grams). Annual production: 50 to 125 eggs.

Special remarks: Australian Spotteds are personable, calm birds that forage well in gardens, which can help duck keepers reduce the numbers of garden pests in their yards. They are also exceptionally hardy with well-developed breast muscles and fine-textured meat. These birds mature quickly and start making courtship displays at three to four weeks of age.

Campbell Duck

Weight of drake: 5½ pounds (2.5 kg)

Weight of female: 4½ pounds (2 kg)

Origin: This strain was developed in England for egg production.

Description: This lightly built but not slim duck has a somewhat upright carriage. There are two color strains: khaki and white. The plumage is the same in both sexes. The khaki strain has a dark brown head and neck with a green luster; the rest of the plumage is khaki with a reddish tinge. The speculum is brown. The white strain is pure white all over.

Eggs: White to greenish. Minimum weight: 2.3 ounces (65 g). Annual production: 180 to 200 eggs.

Special remarks: The Campbell duck is easy to raise, matures early, is hardy and is an enormously productive layer. These qualities make it one of the best utility ducks. Production is highest if the birds have a generous run, but water for swimming is not absolutely necessary.

Magpie Duck

Weight of drake: 5 pounds (2.25 kg)

Weight of female: 4 pounds (1.8 kg)

Origin: The magpie originated in Wales. It is believed to be descended from runner ducks and an old Belgian breed called the Huttegen duck. The magpie is a close relative of the Ancona. The magpie was first imported into the United States in 1963.

Description: As its name implies, the magpie is a black-and-white duck whose markings resemble those of the magpie songbird. The magpie duck is a long-bodied bird with a broad head. In addition to the traditional black-and-white coloration, other color varieties include blue, silver, and chocolate.

Eggs: White. Minimum weight: 2½ ounces (70 g). Annual production: 220 to 290 eggs.

Special remarks: Magpies will help reduce the number of garden pests with their active foraging for food. They also enjoy foraging for grasses, seeds, and aquatic life. Some birds can be high-strung, and magpies can propel themselves over walls up to 3 feet (91 cm) high if startled.

Runner Duck

Weight of drake: 4½ pounds (2 kg)

Weight of female: 4 pounds (1.75 kg)

Origin: This duck goes back to stock from eastern and southeastern Asia with the same upright "penguin" posture. The first runners were brought to England in the 19th century, and many varieties were developed in Germany in the 20th century. It was introduced to the United States around 1900.

Description: The runner is a symmetrically built, trim, slender duck with a very upright carriage. The following color varieties are recognized in the United States: fawn and white, white, penciled, black, buff, chocolate, Cumberland blue, and gray. Other colors found in America include fairy fawn, blue fairy fawn, golden, Saxony, blue fawn, pastel, trout, dusky, khaki, cinnamon, lavender, lilac, blue-brown penciled, blue-fawn penciled, porcelain penciled, and splashed.

Eggs: Mostly white; somewhat greenish in darker strains of birds. Minimum weight: 2.3 ounces (65 g). Annual production: 200 eggs.

Special remarks: This "greyhound" among ducks is very lively and agile, as well as hardy. It is not a meat duck but excels at egg laying. Runners can be bred in confined areas, but the results are much better if the birds have a largish run. They don't need to swim, but they do need a place to bathe. This duck is especially recommended for utility duck breeders in relatively urban environments.

Welsh Harlequin

Weight of drake: 7 pounds (3.1 kg)

Weight of female: 5.5 pounds (2.48 kg)

Origin: The Welsh Harlequin originated in Wales in 1949 when a breeder named Leslie Bonnet paired two mutant light-colored khaki Campbell ducklings. The breed was imported to America in 1968.

Description: Welsh Harlequins are streamlined birds, with longish bodies, round chests, and widely spaced legs. They have trim, oval heads with medium-long, slightly concave bills. Males have greenish black heads, reddish shoulders that are frosted with white, and creamy reddish chestnut breasts. They have multicolored back feathers that provide a tortoise effect in cream, white, brown, and chestnut, and blackish bronze tail feathers that are edged in white. Females have creamy white heads dotted with brown. Their bodies are also creamy white with buff and brownish green or bronze bands on the wings. Females have creamy white and brown tail feathers.

Eggs: White. Minimum weight: 2.3 ounces (65 g). Annual production: 240 to 330 eggs.

Special remarks: Welsh Harlequins are noted for both their egg-laying and meat-producing capabilities. Welsh Harlequins require dry bedding and protection from the elements and from predators. They are placid, docile birds that are good layers and fairly good mothers.

Utility Ducks: Bantamweight Breeds

Call Duck

Weight of drake: 1½ pounds (.75 kg)

Weight of female: 1¼ pounds (0.6 kg)

Origin: This breed was originally developed in England to serve as a decoy in duck hunting.

Description: Weights much over 2 pounds (1 kg) are undesirable. This is a miniature breed with a short body, a round head with full cheeks, a short bill, and a low horizontal carriage. All the colors recognized in large breeds are accepted, both with and without a crest.

Eggs: White to greenish. Minimum weight: 1.4 ounces (40 g). Annual production: about 60 eggs.

Special remarks: This is a very lively and undemanding domestic duck of no economic importance. It can be used to incubate and rear ducklings of ornamental species. It is frequently kept on park waters, where crosses of wild mallards and call ducks are also commonly seen.

East Indie Duck

Weight of drake: 2¼ pounds (1 kg)

Weight of female: 1½ pounds (.75 kg)

Origin: United States. The East Indie was introduced to England around 1850 and was brought to Germany from there.

Description: The East Indie is a small duck with a plump, round body and a slightly raised carriage. The plumage of both sexes is coal black with an iridescent green sheen.

Eggs: Dark green, becoming lighter as the laying season progresses. Minimum weight: 1.9 ounces (55 g). Annual production: up to 80 eggs.

Special remarks: This is an elegant, lively miniature duck of no economic significance. East Indies are kept primarily for esthetic enjoyment. The females incubate and lead their offspring reliably and can therefore be used as foster mothers for ornamental breeds.

Poultry Shows

Poultry shows are an ideal place to learn about ducks. You can meet breeders and see different breeds on display, as well as learn about the fine points of showing a duck in terms of what the judges are looking for and how they classify the birds on display.

As you begin your duck-keeping adventure, a poultry show may provide you with breeder contacts who may be able to supply the birds you need. As your interest and enthusiasm grow, you may find yourself back at the show with birds in tow, ready to compete for points and ribbons.

To learn more about poultry shows, you may want to join the American Poultry Association (for address see page 131) as well as the breed club for the particular duck you wish to show.

Here are some pointers to keep in mind as you prepare for the show:

• Select birds for the show about two weeks prior to the show. This will ensure that you have enough time to prepare the birds for the show.

• When you have selected your show birds, house them in separate cages with clean straw or wood shavings. Keep the cage in a clean, well-ventilated area to acclimate the birds to the show cage.

• Practice moving your show birds in and out of their cages so that you have the procedure down. If you remove the birds from their cages headfirst, it will lessen the chances of damaging the birds' feathers as you remove them from the cage.

• Handle the birds once or twice a day for the two weeks leading up to the show so they will be accustomed to the handling that comes with judging.

• Feed your show birds top-quality feed and fresh water to maintain their good health.

• Show only healthy birds in top condition. These birds must have clean, perfect feathers with bodies that are representative of their breed standard. The birds' feet and faces must also be free of defects and clean. Consult the APA Standard of Perfection (see page 131 for the APA address).

Washing Your Ducks for Show

Wash the birds' feathers several days before taking them to the show. This will give the feathers time to dry and will also give the bird time to groom itself and work natural oils back into the feathers before the show.

Birds with light-colored feathers will need washing more than birds with darker feathers, but you may need to wash darker-colored birds, too, if their feathers are extremely dirty.

To wash just a few birds, you can set up in your sink (for smaller breeds) or bathtub (for larger breeds). Use a recommended detergent that will not dry out feathers and create a soapy lather in the tub. Put the bird in with both hands and hold it securely so that it can't flap its wings. Once the bird's feet are on the tub floor, hold it with only one hand and use the other to work the lather through the bird's feathers. Wash feathers from the bottom to the top to help protect them from breaking.

After you've lathered the bird's feathers, wash its feet gently with a soft toothbrush. Rinse the bird completely (it may be easier to move the bird to another sink or tub that contains clean water, rather than trying to drain the soapy water out while the bird is in it). Be sure to remove all traces of soap so the feathers look smooth and shiny.

Remove the bird from the rinse water and dry it. Remove as much water as you can by hand, then towel them dry by pressing the water out of the feathers. Rubbing the feathers dry is not recommended because it can damage the feathers. Place the birds in cages with clean bedding, which will keep them from getting dirty again before the show.

At the Show

Don't talk to the judges during judging. After the show, judges are more than happy to answer questions you may have, but during the show, they need to stay focused on their judging duties.

Be a gracious winner and an even better loser. No one likes to hear complaints or negative comments at the conclusion of a show. If you lose, congratulate the winner. If you win, humbly accept the congratulations of others.

After the show, keep your show birds separate from the rest of your flock for about two weeks to ensure that no diseases have been brought home from the show to the rest of your ducks.

Ducks in Danger?

According to the American Livestock Breeds Conservancy (ALBC), some duck breeds may be in trouble. The group classifies livestock breeds as critical, rare, watch, study, or recovering, based on the number of breeding pairs in North America. Critical breeds have less than 500 breeding birds and no more than five primary breeding flocks, while rare breeds have less than 1,000 breeding birds and no more than seven primary breeding flocks.

Bird breeds being watched are those with less than 5,000 breeding birds in North America and no more than ten primary breeding flocks. Birds in the study group are those whose breeds are of interest but require definition or historic or genetic documentation. Birds in the recovering category are those that were once listed in another category

and have exceeded more than 5,000 breeding birds in North America.

Here are the ALBC categories for ducks:

Critical: Ancona, Aylesbury, magpie, Saxony, silver Appleyard, Welsh harlequin

Rare: Buff, Cayuga

Watch: Campbell, Rouen, runner, Swedish

Study: Australian Spotted

Recovering: No breeds listed.

Captive duck populations aren't the only ones under scrutiny. A story reported on CNN in mid-2004 stated that, according to the U.S. Fish and Wildlife Service and Canadian Wildlife Service, the wild duck population in the United States and Canada had dropped 11 percent from 2003 (32.2 million birds in 2004 as compared to 36.2 million birds in 2003).

The wildlife services conducted a survey of breeding grounds and said that a shortage of winter precipitation and limited runoff into ponds and basins dried up areas commonly used for breeding.

In the United States, breeding dropped by 7 percent in Montana and the western Dakotas but rose 3 percent in the eastern Dakotas. In some parts of Canada, breeding populations dropped between 4 percent and 9 percent, and in southern Saskatchewan, the population decreased by 38 percent. In northern Manitoba, western Ontario, and northern Saskatchewan, however, populations rose 15 percent.

Chapter Ten

Commercial Uses of Ducks

Meat

Today, domestic ducks are raised almost exclusively for their meat, rather than their eggs and down as in the past. From 1995 to 2000, the per-capita consumption of duck meat, particularly white Pekin duck, has risen more than 20 percent. This rise is attributed to the unique flavor of duck meat, its versatility, and ease of preparation, according to industry leaders. Duck meat is tender, tasty, easily digested, and high in protein. Its fat content and calorie count are comparable to skinless turkey breast.

Fattening Young Ducks

To make the most of the natural early growth spurt and protein production of ducks, duck breeders have moved the fattening period more and more ahead into the first couple of months. Almost all the roast ducks sold are young birds.

When the consumer purchases a duck, he or she expects to get a bird with plenty of breast meat, well-muscled legs, and a generally lean carcass. There should be only a minimum of visible fat accumulation, such as belly fat. As a result of selective breeding, many domestic ducks now have more muscle meat on the breast than on all the rest of the body.

Butchering

The best time to butcher young meat ducks is between nine and ten weeks of age. By that time, the muscles are fully developed. The birds weigh 5 to 5½ pounds (2.2 to 2.5 kg) and haven't yet started their juvenile molt. This last factor is an important one because plucking after slaughter is made much more difficult once lots of new feathers have begun to sprout (see The Molt, a Time of Vulnerability, page 85).

Caution: If you have never butchered animals before, consult an expert. Animal welfare legislation requires that anyone butchering animals have the "necessary knowledge and skills" for the task. If you are lacking in this area, almost any breeder will probably be happy to provide you with sources of information. If you fail to conform to regulations, you may be guilty of animal cruelty.

Recent animal welfare regulations prescribe that warm-blooded animals be stunned before they are bled. A good way to do this is to get a firm hold on the bird's wings with one hand and knock the duck out with a quick, well-aimed blow on the head with a wooden club. Immediately slit the throat just below the head, slicing all the way through to the spinal cord with a single cut of a sharp knife. Let the blood drain from the suspended body. When the carcass is bled, remove the innards through an incision made from the tip of the breastbone to the vent, being careful not to cut into the intestines. Reach into the body cavity with your hand to loosen and remove the internal organs. Save the heart, liver, and gizzard, and dispose of the rest of the viscera to reduce the chances of salmonella contamination.

Dressed Weight

The usable carcass, which includes the neck, wings, and edible internal organs, makes up the dressed weight. In ducks, this is about 75 percent of the live weight. The head, feet, blood, and feathers are considered waste.

Plucking

If you have only a few birds to pluck, either for your own consumption or for sale, you will probably do the job by hand. Large commercial operations use machines that first dry-pick the birds and then strip the carcasses of the last remains of feathers with picking wax. To get rid of the pinfeathers on hand-plucked birds, singe the carcass briefly over a flame.

Although it was once a worthwhile venture, collecting plucked duck feathers is now more of an inconvenience if you have just a few birds because duck feathers and down are imported cheaply and in large quantities from the Far East.

Storage

Most slaughtered ducks are frozen before sale. Freeze the carcasses immediately after butchering in a freezer with an average freezing capacity of at least ⅜ inch (1 cm) per hour. The carcasses should be frozen all the way through to 0°F (−18°C) or colder and should be kept at that temperature.

Eggs

Domestic ducks lay quite a few more eggs than do the mallards from which they descended. Mallards lay only between 7 and 11 eggs a year. Heavy- and medium-weight breeds lay 80 to 130 eggs a year, and breeds developed exclusively for laying, such as the runner and the Campbell duck, accomplish an impressive production of up to 200 eggs a year.

The development of highly productive laying ducks and the realization that duck eggs can play a versatile role in human nutrition led to a significant increase in the number of laying ducks raised in the 1920s and 1930s. But when more and more cases of salmonella poisoning following the consumption of improperly cooked duck eggs occurred in Europe, special regulations controlling the sale of duck eggs were issued. As a result, the consumption of duck eggs dropped dramatically in Europe and America, and they no longer play an economically significant role in the food industries of these countries.

Egg Formation and Egg Laying

Female birds have functioning sexual organs only on the left side of the body. Their reproductive system consists of an ovary and an oviduct.

The ovary, which looks somewhat like a cluster of minute grapes, contains 1,100 to 1,600 egg cells when a duck reaches sexual maturity. These cells start out microscopically small, but some of them, under hormonal stimulation, start to accumu-

late yolks and become enlarged. They are then called ovarian follicles, though they are sometimes also referred to simply as ova.

The oviduct is a long, tubelike organ through which the ovum passes in the process of developing into a complete egg. We distinguish between different parts of the oviduct on the basis of the part each plays in egg formation. At the top is the infundibulum, a funnel-shaped opening; then comes the main section, the albumen-secreting region that creates the egg white; this is followed by the isthmus, the uterus, and, finally, the vagina.

After ovulation, that is, when the mature follicle is released from the ovary, the ovum enters the infundibulum, the funnel-like free end of the oviduct, which lies directly beneath the ovary. Fertilization occurs at this point, assuming copulation has taken place and male gametes are present. The ovum is then moved downward in the oviduct by wavelike muscle contractions (see Egg Binding, page 61). In the next section, the albumen-secreting section, glands contribute 40 to 50 percent of the egg's total amount of egg white.

Shell formation is the next part of the process. Now that the egg—the ovum has developed far enough so that the term egg is more appropriate from this point on—enters a narrow passage in the oviduct, the isthmus, where it absorbs the remaining 50 percent of its albumen as well as the two-layered shell membrane. Later on, an air chamber will form between the inner and the outer membranes. In the uterine section of the oviduct, calcium produced by glands in the oviduct's walls is deposited on the outside of the egg to make a hard shell. Finally, as the egg is about to emerge from the oviduct, it is coated with a secretion from the vagina. This coating dries and hardens only after the egg is laid, forming a skin that seals the pores in the shell, making it impermeable to germs.

When the egg is ready to be laid, the vagina is pushed forward until it protrudes through the cloaca. This protects the egg from contact with bacteria. The laying takes only a few minutes, and the entire process from ovulation to newly laid egg is accomplished in about 24 hours.

Properties

A duck egg differs from a chicken

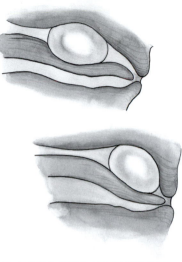

The progression of the egg as it moves through the vagina.

egg by its smooth shell that has a dull sheen and is almost oily.

Weight varies. Eggs of wild mallard ducks average only 1.8 ounces (52.5 g), while eggs of domestic breeds weigh as much as 2.5 ounces (70 g).

Color can also vary. In addition to the familiar white duck eggs, there are often greenish ones; the eggs of Rouen, Pomeranian, and East Indie ducks are often dark green or bluish green.

Here, the vagina protrudes through the cloaca, which protects the egg from harmful bacteria.

Ducks are among the world's most adaptable birds and can be found today in a wide variety of rural and urban settings, including city and community parks.

Fat content is 14.5 percent, compared to 11.6 percent for chicken eggs.

Yolk is pale yellow, if the ducks have been fed primarily potatoes, meals, and grains. If there is more animal protein in the diet, the yolks are lemon to dark yellow. Ducks that have been ranging free and have eaten a lot of acorns sometimes lay eggs with dark brown yolks.

Taste is a matter of discussion. Some people say duck eggs don't taste much different than chicken eggs, while others can definitely tell the difference. Occasionally, duck eggs have a slightly unpleasant rancid or musty taste if the ducks have eaten too many worms, grubs, and snails when foraging.

Cooking properties differ from those of chicken eggs because duck eggs contain more fat in the yolks and more protein in the whites. When whipped, the whites of duck eggs neither become as fluffy as those of chicken eggs nor do they remain as stiff. Also, the white of a duck egg does not become as firm when cooked.

Duck Resources

Organizations and Publications

Following are professional organizations and publications about duck keeping. Contact them for current membership and subscription information.

American Bantam Association
P.O. Box 127
Augusta, NJ 07822
www.bantamclub.com

American Livestock Breeds
Conservancy
P.O. Box 477
Pittsboro, NC 27312
www.albc-usa.org

American Poultry Association
P.O. Box 2209
Mango, FL 33550-2209
www.ampltya.com

Canadian Poultry Magazine
222 Argyle Ave.
Delhi, Ontario N4B 2Y2 Canada
www.canadianpoultrymag.com

Country Smallholding Magazine
Archant Devon
Fair Oak Close
Exeter Airport Business Park
Clyst Honiton
Near Exeter EX5 2UL England
www.countrysmallholding.com

*Gamebird and Conservationists'
Gazette*
Allen Publishing LLC
P.O. Box 171227
Salt Lake City, UT 84117
www.gamebird.com

Hobby Farms magazine
BowTie Inc.
3 Burroughs
Irvine, CA 92618
www.hobbyfarmsmagazine.com

Poultry and Egg News
P.O. Box 1338
Gainesville, GA 30503
www.poultryandeggnews.com

Poultry Press
Attn: Subscriptions
P.O. Box 542
Connersville, IN 47331-0542
www.poultrypress.com

Practical Poultry Magazine
Kelsey Publishing Group
Cudham Tithe Barn
Berry's Hill, Cudham
Kent TN16 3AG England
www.practicalpoultry.co.uk

U.S. Poultry and Egg Association
1530 Cooledge Road
Tucker, GA 30084
www.poultryegg.org

You may also be able to locate information on duck keeping by contacting the poultry science department at your local college or university, or you may be able to obtain information from your Agricultural Extension agent.

For Further Reading

Barnyard in Your Backyard: A Beginner's Guide to Raising Chickens, Ducks, Geese, Rabbits, Goats, Sheep, and Cows by Gail Damerow. Copyright 2002, Storey Books, 210 MASS MoCA Way, North Adams, MA 01247.

Country Life: A Handbook for Realists and Dreamers by Paul Heiney. Copyright 1998, Raincoast Books, 8680 Cambie St., Vancouver, BC, Canada V6P 6M9.

The Domestic Duck by Chris and Mike Ashton. Copyright 2001, Crowood Press, The Stable Block, Crowood Lane, Ramsbury, Wiltshire, SN8 2HR, England.

Domestic Duck and Geese in Colour by Michael Roberts. Copyright 1986, Golden Cockerel Books, Higher Woodbeer, Kennerleigh, Crediton, Devon, EX17 4RS, United Kingdom.

Ducks and Geese at Home by Michael Roberts. Copyright 1998, Golden Cockerel Books, Higher Woodbeer, Kennerleigh, Crediton, Devon, EX17 4RS, United Kingdom.

The Home Farm Handbook by Peter Ford. Copyright 2000, Barron's Educational Series, 250 Wireless Blvd., Hauppauge, NY 11788.

Ortho's All About Building Ponds, Waterfalls and Streams by Charles M. Thomas and Richard M. Koogle. Copyright 2002, Ortho Books, P.O. Box 1749, Columbus, OH 43216.

Storey's Guide to Raising Ducks: Breeds, Care, Health by Dave Holderread. Copyright 2000, Storey Books, 210 MASS MoCA Way, North Adams, MA 01247.

Water Gardens. Copyright 1997, Sunset Books, 80 Willow Road, Menlo Park, CA 94025.

Index

Page numbers in *italic* denote figures.